Beyond Flour

A Fresh Approach to Gluten-Free Cooking & Baking

Enjoy!

Marie Porter

Photography by
Michael Porter

Celebration Generation

www.celebrationgeneration.com

Beyond Flour

First Edition, October 2014

I.S.B.N. 978-0-9846040-6-7

Published and Distributed by

Celebration Generation, LLC
P.O. Box 22315
Robbinsdale, MN 55422

www.celebrationgeneration.com

Cover Photos, Clockwise from Top left:

Ravioli, page 119
Spicy Orange Chicken, page 132
Fruitcake Cookies, page 190
Pita bread, page 66
Doughnut Holes, page 200

Acknowledgments

As always, big thanks got to my husband, Michael Porter First and foremost. Not only for his very tangible contributions to this book - photography, and being a guinea pig for recipe development - but for his unwavering support from day one.

This has been the biggest development project I've ever taken on, and it would not have happened without his constant, steadfast support. Porter, you're amazing.

Not only has this book earned the title of "biggest project", it's also unique for me in another sense - it's by far the most interactive book writing experience I've ever undertaken.

So... thank you to everyone who peer-pressured me into writing this! From the moment I was diagnosed with a gluten allergy, "Will you write a gluten-free cookbook" was the most common question I have been asked ... by friends, fans, and various people on social media. It took a few years to get around to it - if I was going to write this cookbook, it would have to be done RIGHT - but the constant reminders and interest helped fuel the drive to finally take it on. Thank you!

A big part of the "would have to be done RIGHT" was the knowledge that this book would not only be time consuming to develop, it would be expensive. For that reason, we set up a Kickstarter campaign, and hoped for the best. 602 people jumped on board, and here we are!

My sincerest thanks to not only everyone who contributed to the project financially, but also to those who spread the word and encouraged others to have a look at it. I'm still absolutely flabbergasted by the response, and I hope you love the fruits of your generosity!

Special thanks go out in particular to Michelle Bracken, Andrew Deans, Yasin Hakim, Graham and Joyce Orndorff, and Lindy Visaya.

Finally, big thanks to Ben for being my "Haymitch", and helping guide me through one of the weirdest, most traumatic adventures of my life. Who knew it would end up being the final motivation I needed to actually write this book?

Table of Contents

Foreword

Murphy's Law rules my life. This is something that I've known since I was a little kid - seriously, Alanis Morrissette could write a whole sequel to "Ironic" about my life. (Let's face it, that song may not have described irony in any way, but it sure was a Murphy's Law anthem!) Go visit New Orleans for the first time? Trip will be book ended with tropical storms. Buy a house? Get smashed by a tornado just two months after moving in.

No one was really surprised when I ended up diagnosed with a gluten allergy, just MONTHS after opening a cake business.

Some people believe in guardian angels. As a woman of proud Irish heritage, I like to anthropomorphize "Murph" as my guardian leprechaun. He's always there, mischievously throwing curveballs at me, taking me on bizarre side adventures that I never asked for, or wanted.

This isn't as negative as I'm probably making it sound. Those side adventures usually end up being tremendous learning experiences, and end up having silver linings. Murphy's Law has taught me to be prepared for anything - even completely bizarre, nonsensical things that could come up. Life may give me lemons, but hey... I've gotten really good at making lemon curd! Walking down an empty Bourbon St one night in the heaviest rain I've ever seen was a beautiful experience. Serene.. And one of my best memories of the trip!

That tornado was definitely what I call a "character building experience" - at first wryly, eventually warmly and wholeheartedly. I learned a lot about myself, made friends, learned a ton of skills, and was even inspired to write a memoir - Twisted: A Minneapolis Tornado Memoir - about the whole experience.

When it came to the gluten allergy diagnosis, I really didn't see how there could be any silver lining in THAT one. Flour and I had always been the best of friends! I could make ANYTHING with flour, and I did. Our world was filled with the darkest, most beautiful roux, Sunday morning bagels, homemade pretzels, and - of course - cake. In one minute, that was all ripped away from me. I felt betrayed, and life lost a lot of its colour for me, that day.

After trying to get rid of gluten "the easy way" - going Paleo, and not having to worry about all the weird, exotic, and usually expensive flours I'd never dealt with - I decided to give gluten free baking a try. Crustless pizza is NOT pizza, and I wanted PIZZA.

I looked up a few recipes, and tried some of the highest rated ones. There'd be commentary about how you'd never know the difference from full gluten... but in practice, the recipes would always produce something that was not pizza. Cardboard. Gummy textures. Weird tastes and after tastes. A lack of body - I wanted to pick up a slice of pizza, not have to cut it with a knife and fork!

This ended up being a common theme in gluten free recipes I'd try. I soon gave up, and decided to experiment on my own, learning the properties, flavours, and quirks of these new "flours". I started out the way most gluten-free recipes are created - by taking one of my established recipes, and swapping out the flour for special combinations of alternate flours.

This was OK, but never produced anything really spectacular. I realized that in order to really be able to enjoy gluten-free foods, I'd have to completely overhaul the process of gluten-free recipe development.

All my life, I've developed recipes from scratch - both cooking and baking. I guess this could be another example of harnessing Murph.

I'm an Aspie. That is, I am firmly planted in the "Aspergers" section of the autism spectrum. Some call it a disorder, I like to think of it as my superpower... especially in the kitchen. Having ridiculously overdeveloped senses may be annoying at times (bright lights, loud noises)... but it's a huge plus when it comes to cooking. I can tell when the peaches at the grocery store are perfectly ripe, all the way from the deli section. I can replicate pretty much any dish, just from taste and appearance. I can smell when baked goods are ready to come out of the oven.

I bake like I cook, and vice versa. I'd never really seen a difference between cooking and baking, and it's only been recently that I've been exposed to this idea that people are either cooks, or bakers. To me, all cooking and baking is just chemistry and math... balance and proportion. You need a good balance of flavours, body, acid, etc in cooking, you need a balance of structure, leavening, etc in baking. I've always approached it all in the same way I've approached logic problems - in my head.

"If Jenny is twice the age of Bob, who's three years older than Sue..." Really isn't that far off from "I want to make a pizza crust, cannot have gluten in it... but I want THESE properties", in my mind. Baking gluten free recipes from normal recipes by only swapping out the flour is akin to trying to solve the age problem by plugging in the ages of Jennys, Bobs, and Sues that you know in your life.

The thing is, flour is only one ingredient. Recipes aren't about one ingredient, they're about how multiple ingredients AND techniques work together to create a whole. To merely swap out the flour for a set of alternate flours is to ignore all of the ways supporting ingredients - and techniques - can be utilized to create something that you actually want to eat, rather than a mediocre facsimile of what you REALLY want.

The recipes in the book have been developed from the ground up, rather than merely swapping out flour in existing recipes. In some cases, they end up reading and working up fairly close to a "normal" version of the recipe. In others, I've had to get creative with the choices and preparation of the ingredients, yielding recipes that don't look anything like they "should". In all cases, though... it's all about the final product. The food that you will make from the recipes contained in this book will be good food, on its own. You will not need to qualify any compliments with "... for a gluten free dish".

Enjoy!

                                                                 - Marie Porter

Let's Get it Started

While I've mentioned that successful gluten-free cooking/baking isn't just about substituting the flours... having a good working knowledge of what's available, and how to use it is always a good thing.

Every gluten-free flour out there has unique characteristics - protein content, flavour, elasticity, structure, absorption. In my opinion, attempting to combine to just duplicate regular, all purpose flour would do disservice to your final dish.

While all purpose wheat flour is a good, easy catch-all, there are many things that alternate flours do better. When used properly, some will bake up with a crispier texture. Many taste better than regular flour, and most alternate flours are actually more nutritious than wheat flour.

As with all cooking, it's all about balancing flavours and other properties... and proportion. Before you can get to developing your own recipes for gluten-free cooking, it's good to know what those properties are. Here is a bit of an overview:

Name	Type	Notes
Amaranth	Flour	Dense flour with a nutty flavour. Great for savoury breads
Arrowroot	Starch	Commonly used for thickening, like corn starch.
Brown Rice	Flour	Earthy flavour, can be used in place of white rice flour for most uses - it's more nutritious.
Buckwheat	Flour	This is one of the best flours to use in gluten free baking, as it has a neutral taste, and some of the same properties as regular flour - for that reason, many people will skip the use of gums when baking with it. High fibre. I prefer to use "light" or "white" buckwheat, rather than the dark default.
Cassava	Flour	Fairly new to the scene, but often gets confused with tapioca starch, which can be mislabeled as cassava flour. Cassava flour and tapioca starch come from the same plant, but by different processes. Actual cassava flour can be hard to find in local stores.
Coconut	Flour	Sweet, high in fibre.. But soaks up a ton of liquid from your dish. Essential for insanely delicious baked goods, in my opinion!
Corn	Flour	Exactly what it sounds like - flour made from corn! Finely ground, commonly used in Mexican cooking - such as for tamales.
	Meal	Grittier than corn flour. Great for corn muffins, some crusts, etc
	Starch	Primarily used as a thickener, and a starch in baking.
Fava Bean	Flour	High protein flour, with a less aggressive taste than garbanzo bean flour

Garbanzo	Flour	High protein flour, with a slightly bitter taste. Can taste strongly of beans to some people - it's excellent in batters for deep frying. (Chickpea flour)
Garfava	Flour	Combination of Fava bean and Garbanzo bean flours. High protein, mild flavour.
Millet	Flour	One of my favourite flours to work with. Slightly sweet, great for baking with, good nutrition.
Nut , various	Flour	Almost any kind of nut you can imagine is also available as a flour... and you can usually make them at home, also. The "flours" tend to be more "meal" than flour texture, but are great for many uses, especially in cookies. They do add fats to the mix, so keep that in mind when substituting.
Oat	Flour	Heart healthy, much more nutritious than wheat flour. Great tasting - be sure to use certified gluten-free oat flour, to avoid contamination.
Potato	Flour	Used primarily in baking and batters. Can help hold moisture in a recipe.
	Starch	Used as a thickener, can substitute for corn starch for those sensitive to corn
Quinoa	Flour	High in protein, but should be used fairly sparingly - has a strong taste and can make recipes turn out crumbly if used too generously.
Sorghum	Flour	A sweet tasting flour. Great to bake with, and is also commonly used in gluten-free brewing - it behaves closest to wheat flour, of all the alternative flours.
Soy	Flour	AKA kinako (when roasted) flour. Soy is a really common allergen - so I avoid using this one, myself. High protein, dense flour.
Sweet Rice	Flour	Typically found in Asian grocery stores, can also be called "glutenous rice flour" - but don't worry, it does NOT contain gluten. Sweet, and can be used SPARINGLY to add moisture to a dish. (Too much, and it will turn out gummy!)
Tapioca	Starch	Typically used as a thickener (can substitute for corn starch), and to add elasticity and/or a chewy texture to baked goods. Use sparingly - can give a gummy texture.
Teff	Flour	By far, Teff is best known for its use in Injera - a stretchy African bread. It's great for adding a bit of elasticity to a recipe. As with most gluten-free flours, it definitely works best in conjunction with other flours. (It lacks the strength to hold up most baked good recipes, etc)
White Rice	Flour	A really common flour in GF cooking, but it definitely needs supporting ingredients - it doesn't hold together well on its own, leading to crumbly consistencies. White rice flour is a great addition to deep fried batters, as it can produce a crispier texture.
Wild Rice	Flour	Should be used sparingly, as it has a very aggressive taste. (Earthy, almost gamey!)/ Can be used as a thickener, or to add flavour to savoury baked goods and other dishes.

It would be really unreasonable to expect anyone to acquire - and keep fresh! - every variety of gluten-free flour out there. For the purposes of this book, I kept the working flours limited to:

Amaranth Flour
Brown Rice Flour
Buckwheat Flour (white/light!)
Coconut Flour
Corn flour, Meal, and Starch
Garbanzo flour
Millet Flour
Oat Flour
Potato Flour
Potato Starch
Sorghum Flour
Sweet Rice Flour
Tapioca Starch
White Rice Flour

... yes, that still looks like a lot, I know - but it's worth it, I promise!

I recommend looking through the recipes, picking a few you're interested in, and seeing what flours are called for across them. As an example, I pretty much only use garbanzo flour for deep fried items, and tend to only use coconut flour for baked goods.

From there, I'd vote for going online and placing an order for a small bag - about 1 lb - of each of the flours you see yourself using. Get some nice canisters to keep them in - I bought tall glass ones at IKEA - and clearly label them.

After the first order of flours, you'll be able to develop a good idea of what you go through fastest, and what you should buy in bigger quantities. As an example, I always buy the sorghum and white buckwheat flours in 5lb bags, but I go through coconut flour fairly slowly - most recipes only call for 1/4 cup!

Anyway...

 Beyond knowing what the flours taste like, and what they're good for.. Tweaking your recipe techniques go a long way to increasing your success in gluten-free cooking and baking. Here are a few things to keep in mind, as you work through this book:

Absorption: The various alternate flours absorb liquid at different rates. Experiment with this, and learn to use it to your advantage. As an example, coconut flour sucks moisture out of a recipe far more than most other flours.

Additionally, absorption can affect the way you should handle certain flours. You know how you should soak dried beans in water overnight, before working with them? Well, that same thing applies to bean flours, also - generally speaking, you'll want to mix them into the liquid and let it stand for 10 minutes or so to soften, before proceeding with the recipe. It softens the flour, and makes a big difference to the texture of the final product!

Humidity can also be a concern with gluten-free baking. The alternative flours can be far more finicky than wheat flour, when it comes to liquids and humidity. If you live in a humid area/house.. You may want to decrease the moisture content in your recipe, if even just slightly. Experiment!

Expectations: Non-gluten flours behave differently than regular gluten flour. Even when a dish is going to turn out to be a VERY close match for the original, full-gluten version... it may not act like it, up til that point. That's ok!

Your bread dough will be more like cake batter, than something you'd knead by hand. The base recipe I came up with to batter and deep fry foods is VERY thick, kind of goopy, and not quite as easy to dip in, as regular flour. It's all good - and it'll work out well in the end. Just don't expect it to work up in exactly the same way as you're used to!

Fermentation: While some gluten-sensitive people have no problems with gluten that has been fermented - soy sauce, beer, even some sourdough bread! - I recommend using gluten free beers and soy sauces whenever possible, ESPECIALLY if it's a matter of being Celiac. (VS autoimmune sensitivity, etc).

Moisture: One main problem with gluten-free baking is that things can turn out to be dry and/or crumbly if you're not careful. Adding a ton of liquid to a recipe isn't always the best idea, as it will reduce the structural integrity. So, it's good to be sneaky about it.

Use moist, non-liquid ingredients to boost and hold the moisture in a dish. Think pureed fruit like applesauce, extra eggs, dried fruit, honey, yogurt, and/or sour cream. These items can be used to add great flavour and texture to the final dish, in addition to being a moisture solution. The fruitcake cookies on page 190 are one of my absolute favourite cookies ever - even counting full-gluten cookies!

Oats: Oats are a sticky issue for some. The Canadian Celiac Association has declared oats to be safe for consumption, so long as they're uncontaminated. I've never had a reaction, myself... and I love using oats and oat flours in my gluten-free baking. They taste great - much better than wheat flour - and they're heart healthy! However, just be sure that when you're using oats, that you're using oats that are certified gluten-free, just to be safe!

Structure: The main property of wheat flour that can be lacking in alternate flours is the strength to hold up to certain types of baking - cakes, breads, etc.
When it comes to breads, and bread like baking, you'll want to make sure to have a decent amount of protein in the recipe (whether from the alternate flours, eggs, or a combination thereof), as well as an ingredient(s) that act as a binder or glue. This can come from gums - commonly either xanthan or guar - and/or use of a sticky starch, such as tapioca starch.

When it comes to cakes, quick breads, etc ... I like to use eggs for both protein supplementation and structure. Separating the eggs and whipping the whites to a stiff peak before folding into your cake batter goes a long way to providing the structure a cake needs to rise and *stand*. It's a bit more work - and dishes! - than the usual of just tossing whole eggs into the batter, but it makes a ton of difference to the final product.

One of the major complaints about gluten-free cooking is having to use "many" flours, and the expense involved with getting set up. I've found it's really best to look at them as individual ingredients, rather than a whole bunch of substitutions for one ingredient. Think of it like having a well stocked spice cabinet. Sure, the up-front expense stings a bit.. But upkeep isn't that bad, refilling as you need. Also, a well stocked spice rack makes cooking a LOT more fun - and tasty - than only having salt and pepper on hand!

A Note on Measuring

The way you measure your flours can impact the amount of flour that you get in any given measurement. Some people scoop, others spoon. Some level off with a flat edge, others shake off the excess. Some believe that how you measure will GREATLY impact how your recipe turns out, I happen to think that if you use the same technique for all of it, it'll come out fine - no need to stress.

If you're interested, these recipes were all developed by using the measuring cup to scoop the flour, tapping it off the side of the container to shake off excess / level what's in there.

A Note on Equipment

Generally speaking, these recipes will just require basic cooking equipment - bowls, measuring spoons/cups, pots, pans, and basic bakeware. A few require a specialty piece: a waffle iron, for instance. I've done my best to only include specialty equipment when it's something you'll probably get a lot of use out of (waffle iron), or are super cheap (English muffin rings)

The one big exception? A lot of these recipes mention using a food processor. If there is one piece of equipment that will make your life easier in the kitchen, it is a food processor. Even if you pick up a secondhand one for next to nothing, I HIGHLY recommend it. Trust me on this.

If you don't have a food processor, there are other ways to achieve the same sort of thing.

For instances where a food processor is being used to make dough, you can mix it by hand, use a stand mixer, or use an electric hand mixer.

For instances where a food processor is being used to chop something, you can chop it by hand.

For instances where a food processor is being used to puree something, you can use a blender. When there is not a lot of liquid involved, you'll want to do it in very small batches, however.

Let's get to the recipes now..

Breakfast & Brunch

Potato Pancakes

I've loved potato pancakes ever since I was a kid. Despite my raging sweet tooth, I preferred their savouriness to more traditional pancake options, and loved loading them up with sour cream and sliced green onions.

Makes about 4 servings

Large red potatoes, peeled.	2-3	2-3
Small onion, grated	1/2	1/2
Salt	1 tsp	5 ml
Light buckwheat flour	2/3 cup	150 ml
Sorghum flour	1/3 cup	75 ml
Tapioca starch	1 Tbsp	15 ml
Baking soda	1/2 tsp	2 ml
Large eggs	3	3
Milk	1/4 cup	50 ml
Pepper	1/2 tsp	2 ml
Parsley, chopped	1/4 cup	50 ml
Cooking spray		

Shred potato, measuring out 4 cups - discard any extra. In a large bowl, combine shredded potato with shredded onion, toss to combine. Add salt, toss once more to combine. Allow to stand undisturbed for 10 minutes.

While waiting, combine flours, starch, and baking soda in a large bowl. Add eggs, milk, pepper, and parsley, stir gently until just combined.

Once 10 minutes is up, squeeze out extra liquid from the potato mixture, and add it to the batter, stirring gently to distribute the potatoes evenly through the batter.

Spray griddle or frying pan with cooking spray, heat to medium or medium-low heat. Scoop 1/4 cup amounts of batter onto the griddle. Gently spread batter out into a larger circle, about 4 – 4.5" in diameter. Cook until bubbles start popping through top surface. Flip, cook until done.

Serve with apple sauce and/or sour cream, and green onion slices.

Potato Pancakes

Apple Streusel Muffins

A while back - in my pre-gluten-free days - I went one a big muffin making kick. I'd make all kinds of muffins, a different flavour each week - partridgeberry, raspberry-nectarine, cardamom-pear... and they'd serve as breakfasts for the week. Once going gluten-free, I knew I'd need to come up with a great fruit-based muffin recipe - I'd never had a great gluten-free muffin!

Fruit is an excellent way to add some more flavour AND nutrition in any muffin - gluten or not - but when it comes to gluten-free muffins, the moisture that fruit adds is key to a great texture!

Light buckwheat flour	1/2 cup	125 ml
Sorghum flour	1/2 cup	125 ml
Gluten-free oat flour	3/4 cup	175 ml
Potato flour	1/4 cup	50 ml
Tapioca starch	1/4 cup	50 ml
Light brown sugar, packed	1/2 cup	125 ml
Granulated sugar	1/2 cup	125 ml
Baking powder	2 tsp	10 ml
Cinnamon	1 tsp	5 ml
Salt	1/2 tsp	2 ml
Baking soda	1/4 tsp	1 ml
Large eggs	2	2
Milk	3/4 cup	175 ml
Butter, melted	1/2 cup	125 ml
Grated apple	1 1/2 cups	375 ml
Vanilla extract	1 tsp	5 ml
Gluten-free oat flour	1/4 cup	50 ml
Granulated sugar	1/4 cup	50 ml
Cinnamon	1/2 tsp	1 ml
Butter	2 Tbsp	30 ml

Preheat oven to 375 F (190 C). Line 12 muffin cups with liners, or spray with baking spray.

In a large bowl, combine flours, tapioca starch, sugars, baking powder, cinnamon, salt, baking soda, Make a well in center of flour mixture; set aside.

In another bowl, combine eggs, milk, melted butter, grated apple, and vanilla extract. Add wet mixture all at once to the flour mixture. Stir just until moistened (batter should be lumpy.) Divide batter between 12 prepared muffin cups, filling each to almost full.

In small bowl, mix together flour, sugar, and cinnamon. Use a pastry cutter or two forks to cut in butter until the mixture resembles coarse crumbs. Sprinkle streusel topping over muffin batter in cups.

Bake for 18 to 20 minutes or until golden and a wooden toothpick inserted in centers comes out clean. Cool in muffin cups on a wire rack for 5 minutes. Remove from muffin cups; serve warm. Makes 12 muffins.

Variations:

Cardamom Pear: Substitute grated pear for the grated apple, and cardamom in place of the cinnamon.

Peach & Pecan: Substitute peach for the apple, and pecan meal (or other favourite nut meal - walnut works great!) for the oat flour in the struesel.

Apple Streusel Muffins

English Muffins

While traditional English muffins can be made with or without a muffin ring, doing it gluten-free requires English muffin rings. In order to get the right texture from a gluten-free dough, you need a lot more liquid in the batter than will allow the muffins to stand on their own in a raw form. English muffin rings are available online, and in many cooking stores. I purchased a set on Amazon for about $5.

Makes about 6 muffins

Warm - not hot - water	1/2 cup	125 ml
Sugar	2 tsp	10 ml
1 packet instant yeast	2 1/4 tsp	11 ml
White rice flour	1/2 cup	125 ml
Potato starch	1/2 cup	125 ml
Sorghum flour	1/2 cup	125 ml
Light buckwheat flour	1/2 cup	125 ml
Tapioca starch	1/4 cup	50 ml
Xanthan gum	1 tsp	5 ml
Salt	1 tsp	5 ml
Warm milk	3/4 cup	175 ml
Shortening, melted	1/4 cup	50 ml
Large eggs, beaten	2	2
Baking powder	1 tsp	5 ml
Cornmeal		
Cooking spray		

Combine warm water with sugar, stirring until sugar is almost dissolved. Add yeast, stirring until incorporated. Cover bowl with plastic wrap. Set aside in a warm place for 10 minutes, or until foamy.

In a very large mixing bowl, combine flours, tapioca starch, xanthan gum and salt, whisking until well combined. Add warm milk and melted shortening, once again stirring until combined. Add water/yeast mixture, once again whisking until fully combined. Loosely cover bowl with plastic wrap, leave out on the counter overnight - at least 8 hours.

Preheat oven to 350 F (190 C). Line baking sheet with parchment paper, and scatter with cornmeal. Coat 6 English muffin rings liberally with cooking spray, then arrange on the pan.

Whisk eggs and baking powder into fermented dough, making sure it well incorporated.

Line pan with parchment, scatter cornmeal evenly across it. Place 6 English muffin rings on it. Divide the batter between the rings, scatter more cornmeal on top. Set aside in a warm spot for 20 minutes.

Carefully slip a spatula under one muffin ring to transfer rings - batter and all - to a greased griddle, one at a time. Cook English muffins over medium heat - still in the ring - for a minute or two on each side, just long enough for it to brown up a little and form a bit of a crust.

Carefully transfer back to baking sheet, remove rings. Bake for 30-35 minutes, or until cooked through. Serve hot.

English Muffins

Quiche

Quiche is one of those things that I never really make the same way twice... so settling on what I was going to include for the filling part of the recipe was kind of difficult. The possibilities are endless! So, here's a good basic recipe. Feel free to play with it, swapping out the meats, veggies, and cheeses to suit your tastes, or what you have on hand.

Sorgham flour	3/4 cup	175 ml
White rice flour	3/4 cup	175 ml
Sweet rice flour	1/4 cup	50 ml
Millet flour	1/2 cup	125 ml
Tapioca starch	1 Tbsp	15 ml
Corn starch	1/4 cup	50 ml
Salt	1/2 tsp	2 ml
Baking powder	1/2 tsp	2 ml
1 brick cream cheese, softened	8 oz	250 g
Butter, softened	1/2 cup	125 ml
Water	1 Tbsp	15 ml
Corn starch, for rolling	~1/4 cup	~ 50 ml
Thick cut bacon, chopped	1 lb	500 g
Medium onion, thinly sliced	1	1
Garlic	1 clove	1 clove
Mushrooms	8 oz	250 g
Baby spinach	3 cups	750 ml
Large eggs	7	7
Heavy cream	1 1/2 cups	375 ml
Grated Swiss cheese	1 1/2 cups	375 ml
Salt and pepper, to taste		

Measure all dry ingredients into a food processor, blitz a couple of times to combine. Add cream cheese, butter, and water. Run the food processors just long enough to pull mixture together into a dough. Wrap dough tightly in plastic wrap, chill for 20 minutes.

Generously dust your work surface with corn starch, roll out dough into a circle big enough for your 13" quiche pan. Gently transfer dough to quiche pan, pressing edges of dough into the fluted edge of the pan. Cover and chill until ready to bake.

Preheat oven to 425F (220 C)

In a large pan, cook bacon until almost crispy. Strain bacon off, leaving drippings in the pan. Set bacon aside. Saute onion, garlic, and mushrooms in bacon drippings, until tender. Add spinach, continue cooking until well wilted. Add bacon, stir to combine, and strain off any remaining drippings. Allow to cool. In a separate bowl, whisk eggs and heavy cream together. Add Swiss cheese and cooled bacon mixture. Pour into prepared shell. Bake 30-40 minutes, covered in foil. Remove foil for last 10 minutes of baking time. Serve hot

.

Quiche

Popular Toaster .. Tarts?

Toaster pastries are one of those things that satisfy some weird need for childhood comfort food every once in a while... even though they aren't actually really that good. It's funny how many people brought them up as one of the foods they miss most, when going gluten-free!

These are actually BETTER than the original source material.. and far better for you. Firm but slightly chewy dough base, your choice of filling, and freshly made frosting. Garnish the top any way you want - even sprinkles - and just have fun with it.

One word of warning, though: Without the source material chemicals and stabilizers, the frosting on these ones is actually fairly heat sensitive, and will melt when toasted. So, use in a toaster oven rather than a traditional "pop up" style toaster... or turn your normal toast on it's side, and toast them frosting-side up...Keeping an eye out for drippage!

Makes about 10

Brown rice flour	1 cup	250 ml
Sorghum flour	1 cup	250 ml
Gluten-free oat flour	1/4 cup	50 ml
Coconut flour	1/4 cup	50 ml
Tapioca starch	2 Tbsp	30 ml
Xanthan gum	2 tsp	10 ml
Baking powder	1/2 tsp	2 ml
Salt	1/2 tsp	2 ml
Granulated sugar	2/3 cup	150 ml
Butter, melted	1/2 cup	125 ml
Vanilla	1 tsp	5 ml
Milk	1/2 cup	125 ml
Large eggs, separated	2	2
Seedless jam of choice	1 cup	250 ml
Corn starch	1 Tbsp	15 ml

Preheat oven to 350 F (180 C). Line a cookie sheet with parchment paper.

Whisk together the dry ingredients until well combined. In a separate bowl, whisk together all wet ingredients, except for one of the two eggs. Add wet ingredients to the dry, mix until a thick dough forms. Wrap in plastic, chill for 30 minutes.

Roll dough out to about slightly thinner than 1/4" thick, cut into 3x5" rectangles. Gather any scraps, needs to pull together, re roll and continue cutting into rectangles until all the dough is used up.

Carefully arrange half of the rectangles on the cookie sheet, spaced evenly. Whisk jam and corn starch together until well combined. Evenly spread about 2 Tbsp of filling onto each of the rectangles on the cookie sheet, stopping about 1/2" from the edges. Top each with one of the reserved rectangles, press the edges to seal. Use a fork to press edges down.

Whisk egg together with 1 Tbsp cold water, brush over each pastry. Use a fork to prick a few small holes in the top of each pastry to allow steam to escape - this will help prevent filling from exploding out of the sides as they bake

Bake pastries for about 15 minutes, until golden brown. Cool completely before removing from the cookie sheet.

Frosting:

Icing (powdered) sugar	1 1/2 + cups	375+ ml
Hot water	2 Tbsp	30 ml
vanilla extract	1/2 tsp	2 ml
food colouring, if desired.		

Whisk powdered sugar, water, and vanilla extract together - frosting will be THICK. Microwave for 10-20 seconds to melt, stir until smooth. Spread onto pastries, garnish with sprinkles if using.

Allow frosting to dry fully, before transferring to containers or baggies. Serve hot or room temperature, use or freeze within a few days of baking.

Toaster Pastries

Banana Bread

I've always been known for my banana bread recipe - it's a tweaked version of my grandma's recipe, and it's fabulous. It's always daunting to try and improve on borderline perfection, especially when doing something major - such as removing the gluten. It took a couple of tries, but I'm pleased to report that this recipe is at least as good as that original recipe - more nutritious, too!

As with the original, is a great base recipe... and begging to be customized to your preferences. Use raisins, or don't. Use dried cranberries, or walnuts, or whatever else you'd like in banana bread... or just leave the extras out entirely, and enjoy it as a plain – but SO tasty! – banana bread.

Oh, and it's easy, too … you can make this in a bowl, with a wooden spoon. No mixer required!

Light buckwheat flour	1/2 cup	125 ml
Millet or gluten-free oat flour	1/2 cup	125 ml
Sorghum flour	1/2 cup	125 ml
Tapioca starch	2 Tbsp	30 ml
Baking soda	1 tsp	5 ml
Salt	1/2 tsp	2 ml
Large bananas, mashed*	3	3
Butter, melted	1/4 cup	50 ml
Large eggs	2	2
Granulated sugar	1 cup	250 ml
Nuts and/or raisins, optional **		

Preheat oven to 375 F (190 C). Grease 1 regular/large loaf pan, or about 3 mini loaf pans.

Whisk together flours, tapioca starch, baking soda, and salt. Set aside.

Mix together bananas, butter, egg and sugar until smooth. Add flour mixture, and nuts and/or raisins if you'll be using them. Mix just until everything is well combined.

Pour batter into greased pan. Bake for about 1 hour, or until crust is a rich golden brown, and knife inserted into middle of loaf comes out clean.

Serve warm, or cooled. Best served within 2-3 days.

* Use VERY ripe bananas. If you have bananas that are perfectly (over!) ripe for banana bread, but need to hold off on actually making it… just toss them in the freezer. The peel will go black, the the bananas will be perfect!

** I like a ton of raisins, and will usually use about 1 cup of dark raisins. As far as nuts go, I prefer walnut, but feel free to substitute. Use 1/2 – 1 cup of nuts, or 1/2 cup each of nuts and raisins. Have fun with it!

Banana Bread

Waffles

Homemade waffles were a new thing to me, when going gluten-free. I'd only ever had waffles when served in a restaurant - making them at home seemed like too much of a hassle to bother. Plus, I'm not really a "breakfast food" kind of person.

WELL. Let me tell you, one of the first things you should buy when going gluten-free is a waffle maker. They don't have to be expensive OR take up a lot of space, and should definitely be considered an exemption to the "no kitchen appliances that have only one specific use" idea. Not only are gluten-free waffles easy to make, the nature of waffles - and a waffle maker - make them an ideal substitution for breakfast breads. The waffle maker will make the outside of your waffles crispy, and - with a good recipe! - the insides will be fluffy and tender. It hits all the notes that I missed, in regular bread.. without the wait of making bread.

I couldn't restrain myself to just one waffle recipe - they're each so great, and SO adaptable to different toppings, etc.. I'd like to provide some options.

Basic Waffles

I like this basic waffle recipe as a base for a sweet topping - fruit, syrup, or - as pictured - "ambrosia waffles".

Makes ~ 6 Belgian style waffles

White rice flour	3/4 cup	175 ml
Buttermilk	1 3/4 cups	425 ml
Large eggs	3	3
Potato starch	1/2 cup	125 ml
Sorghum flour	1/4 cup	50 ml
Coconut flour	1/4 cup	50 ml
Tapioca starch	1/4 cup	50 ml
Baking powder	2 tsp	10 ml
Salt	1 tsp	5 ml
Granulated sugar	1 tsp	5 ml
Vegetable oil	1/4 cup	50 ml

Whisk together white rice flour, buttermilk, and eggs, allow to sit for 5 minutes.

In a separate bowl, whisk together remaining dry ingredients until well combined. Add dry ingredients to buttermilk mixture along with vegetable oil, whisk until well combined. Allow to sit for 5 minutes before using.

Follow your waffle iron instructions to cook the waffles. Serve hot!

Ambrosia Waffles

In my hometown - Winnipeg, Manitoba - I used to order these waffles any time we went to the breakfast restaurant up the street. Having not had access to that for YEARS, ambrosia waffles were literally the first thing on my mind when I ordered my new waffle maker. SO good!

Cream cheese, room temperature	8 oz	250 g
Milk	1/2 cup	125 ml
Granulated sugar	1 Tbsp	15 ml
Salt	1/2 tsp	2 ml
Fresh strawberries, sliced		
Banana, sliced		

In a small saucepan, carefully whisk together softened cream cheese with milk until smooth. Add sugar and salt, whisk once more to combine. Heat just to a simmer, whisking constantly to dissolve the sugar. Spread cream cheese sauce over hot waffles, top with strawberry and banana slices.

Ambrosia Waffles

Sourdough Waffles

I love these waffles as a more savoury alternative to my basic waffles recipe. While you could absolutely use them as a base for fruit, I prefer to compliment the tang of the sourdough with savoury toppings.

Going outside of the box, this is a great substitute for bread - these BLT sandwiches were amazing, but I'll even pop a batch on when I miss sourdough bread, and just eat them straight out of the waffle iron.

These are made in two parts - the "starter" is made the night before use. When ready to use, a couple more ingredients are whisked in, and you're ready to go!

Warm - not hot - water	1 cup	250 ml
Granulated sugar	1 tsp	5 ml
Active dry yeast (or one packet)	2 1/2 tsp	12 ml
Brown rice flour	1 cup	250 ml
Gluten-free oat flour	1/2 cup	125 ml
Amaranth flour	1/4 cup	50 ml
Millet flour	1/4 cup	50 ml
Tapioca starch	2 Tbsp	30 ml
Salt	1 tsp	5 ml
Warm milk	1 1/2 cups	375 ml
Butter, melted	1/2 cup	125 ml
Large eggs	2	2
Baking soda	1/2 tsp	2 ml

To make your starter the night before:

Combine warm water with sugar, stirring until sugar is almost dissolved. Add yeast, stirring until incorporated. Loosely cover bowl with plastic wrap. Set aside in a warm place for 10 minutes, or until foamy.

In a very large mixing bowl, combine flours, tapioca starch, and salt, whisking until well combined. Add warm milk and melted butter, once again stirring until combined. Add water/yeast mixture, once again whisking until fully combined. Loosely cover bowl with plastic wrap, leave out on the counter overnight - at least 8 hours.

When ready to use, heat up your waffle iron. Whisk eggs together with baking soda, then whisk that mixture into your "starter".

Follow your waffle iron instructions to cook the waffles. Serve hot!

Sourdough Waffles

Cornbread waffles

Along the lines of my sourdough waffles, I tend to look at my cornbread waffles less as actual WAFFLES, and more of a quick and lazy way to make bread. When it comes to cornbread, waffles are ALL about the instant gratification! I love the texture that the waffle maker imparts on what could have been a more traditional serving of corn bread.

Masa harina	1 cup	250 ml
Yellow cornmeal	1/2 cup	125 ml
Tapioca starch	1/4 cup	50 ml
Baking powder	2 tsp	10 ml
Salt	1 tsp	5 ml
Granulated sugar	1 Tbsp	15 ml
Buttermilk	1 1/2 cups	375 ml
Vegetable oil	1/4 cup	50 ml
Large eggs	2	2

In a large bowl, whisk together dry ingredients until well combined. In a separate bowl, whisk together buttermilk, oil, and eggs until smooth.

Pour wet ingredient mixture into bowl of dry ingredients, whisk until well combined. Allow to sit for 10 minutes before using. Follow your waffle iron instructions to cook the waffles. Serve hot!

Cornbread Waffles

Crepes

Much like waffles, crepes are a great way to fill that bread void. This recipe can be made either sweet or savoury, and can be topped or filled with pretty much anything you can think of.

While you CAN make crepes on the stove top.. well, I have a confession to make: I am monumentally bad at making pancakes. I mean, I can make any of the fanciest pastries you can think of, but literally have to have my husband actually cook pancakes for me. (I make the batter, though!). When it came to making crepes at home, I was terrified of the idea of making GIANT, really thin pancakes... so I wussed out and bought a crepe maker.

Definitely recommend that strategy. It's just a plug in, round cook top that you can use on the counter. It has a slight lip to prevent the batter from pouring out everywhere, but it's not so high that it makes flipping them problematic. It's uniform heat, so they cook up beautifully.

Makes about 8 crepes

Sorghum flour	1/2 cup	125 ml
White rice flour	1/4 cup	50 ml
Tapioca starch	1/4 cup	50 ml
Salt	1/4 tsp	1 ml
Milk	1 cup	250 ml
Water	1/4 cup	50 ml
Large eggs	2	2 ml
Butter, melted	1/4 cup	50 ml
Pan spray		

In a large mixing bowl, whisk together all dry ingredients until well combined.

In a separate mixing bowl, whisk together milk, water, eggs, and melted butter. Pour into the dry ingredients, whisk until smooth and well combined, with no lumps. Allow to sit for 5 minutes before using.

Over medium heat, heat a nonstick frying pan or griddle. Pour about 1/4 cup (50 ml) of batter onto the pan, swirling the pan to spread the batter into a large, VERY thin, even circle.

Cook for a minute or two before, until bottom of crepe starts to brown. Carefully flip, cook for 1 more minute. Continue until all of the batter is used up.

Variations:

- Sweet crepes: Add 2 Tbsp (30 ml) granulated sugar to the dry ingredients, and 1 tsp (5 ml) vanilla to the wet ingredients

- Spread crepe with Nutella, sprinkle with banana and strawberry slices, and roll up!

- Add finely chopped fresh herbs to the dry ingredients, fill prepared crepes with cheese.

- Roll together with sliced deli meats and cheeses, for a fancy sandwich roll

Mushroom Swiss Crepes with Asparagus:

Mushrooms, sliced	1 lb	500 g
Small onion, chopped	1/2	1/2
Clove garlic, pressed	1	1
Olive oil	1 Tbsp	15 ml
Salt and pepper		

In a large frying pan or wok, saute the mushrooms, onion, and garlic in olive oil until tender. Season with salt and pepper, to taste. Serve with blanched asparagus spears, and Swiss cream sauce:

Butter	1/4 cup	50 ml
White rice flour	1/4 cup	50 ml
White wine	1 cup	250 ml
Shredded Swiss cheese	2 cups	500 ml
Milk	2 cups	500 ml
Salt and pepper		

In a medium saucepan, melt butter. Whisk in rice flour, cook over medium heat for two minutes.

Slowly add white wine, whisking as you pour. Once wine is fully incorporated and smooth, add Swiss cheese and milk, stirring until everything is melted and well combined. Season with salt and pepper, to taste.

Mushroom Swiss Crepes with Asparagus

Banana Buckwheat Pancakes with Blueberry Syrup

Much like with my muffin recipe (Page 17), I like to use fruits to add flavour, nutrition, and moisture to my pancakes. These banana buckwheat pancakes are stellar - they have a hearty texture without being obnoxious, and a great flavour. Combined with fresh blueberry sauce, it's a fantastic meal to start the day off with!

Makes about 8 pancakes

Light buckwheat flour	2/3 cup	150 ml
Sorghum flour	1/3 cup	75 ml
Brown sugar, packed	1/4 cup	50 ml
Baking powder	1 1/2 tsp	7 ml
Salt	1/4 tsp	1 ml
Buttermilk*	3/4 cup	175 ml
Large bananas, mashed	2	2
Vanilla	1/2 tsp	2 ml
Large egg	1	1
Vegetable oil	1 Tbsp	15 ml
Blueberry syrup, recipe below		

In a bowl, combine flours, brown sugar, baking powder, and salt. Set aside. In blender, process buttermilk, banana, vanilla, egg, and oil until smooth. Pour into dry ingredients. Lightly stir, just until combined - do not over beat it!

Lightly oil your griddle or frying pan, preheat over medium or medium-low heat. Scoop 1/4 cup (50 ml) amounts of batter onto the griddle. Gently spread batter out into a larger circle, about 4 – 4.5" in diameter. Cook until bubbles start popping through top surface. Flip, cook until done.

Serve with blueberry syrup... maybe with whipped cream, and a sprinkling of nutmeg!

*If not buttermilk, use 1 1/2 cups (375 ml) milk, with 1 tbsp (15 ml) lemon juice mixed in. Allow to sit for 5 minutes before using.

Blueberry syrup

1 pack frozen blueberries	12 oz	340 g
Granulated sugar	1 cup	250 ml
Salt	1/2 tsp	2 ml
Water*	1/4 cup	50 ml
Zest of one orange		

Combine all ingredients in a medium saucepan. Bring to a boil over medium-high heat, stirring constantly. Once boiling, reduce heat to medium-low and simmer for 5 minutes or until thickened.

* For a more "adult" variation, substitute Amaretto for the water!

Banana Buckwheat Pancakes with Blueberry Syrup

Madeleines

Madeleines are a traditional tea cake – almost a cookie – from northeastern France. While there are several different variants of flavour for the cakes, one thing is pretty much constant – the shape. Madeleines are baked using a special pan with shallow, shell shaped indentations. Very pretty! Madeleine pans can be purchased at many department and home goods stores, or online.

Coconut flour	1/3 cup	75 ml
White rice flour	1/3 cup	75 ml
Sorghum flour	1/3 cup	75 ml
Potato starch	1/3 cup	75 ml
Tapioca starch	1 1/2 Tbsp	22 ml
Baking powder	2 tsp	10 ml
Large eggs, separated	5	5
Granulated sugar	1 cup	250 ml
Butter, melted	1/2 cup	125 ml
Zest and juice of 1 lemon		
Salt pinch		

Preheat oven to 400 F (200 C). Generously grease Madeleine pan with shortening.

Whisk together flours, starches, and baking powder. If you're a purist, you can also sift them at this point - I don't bother. Set aside.

In a stand mixer, whisk egg whites until soft peaks form. Set aside.

In a separate bowl, combine egg yolks and sugar, beat until pale yellow. Add butter, lemon juice and zest, mix until well combined. Add dry ingredients to mixing bowl of wet ingredients, stir until well incorporated and smooth. Gently fold into whipped egg whites, stirring until completely incorporated.

Spoon 1 Tbsp (15 ml) of batter into each prepared Madeleine mold cavity. Bake for 10-12 minutes, or until golden. Turn Madeleines out onto a clean dishtowel, cool.

To serve, dust Madeleines with a little powdered sugar, or dip 1 end/side of each shell into melted chocolate.

Madeleines

Baking Powder Biscuits

When I was a kid, I always looked forward to my grandmother's baking powder biscuits. We'd eat them with butter and lots of homemade jam, and life was good.

It was a recipe that doesn't need tweaking...until I found out I'd need to stop eating wheat. It took some fussing, but I'm happy to be able to finally present you with a delicious, perfect texture biscuit recipe!

This recipe can be played with a bit, depending on what you're in the mood for, and what you have on hand. Sometimes I'll use milk (as she did), sometimes I'll use buttermilk. If I don't have shortening (as she used) or if I want a richer flavour, I'll use butter instead. It's all good! As long as you don't over-handle the dough, these biscuits bake up light and fluffy, and are easily split in half. This makes about 6 good sized biscuits, but is easily doubled.

Makes 6 biscuits

Light buckwheat flour	1 cup
Millet flour	3/4 cup
Potato flour	1/4 cup
Tapioca starch	2 tsp
Baking Powder	3 tsp
Salt	1 tsp
Shortening or butter	1/3 cup
Milk or buttermilk	1 1/4 cup

Preheat oven to 450 F (230 C). Spray a baking sheet with nonstick spray, or line with parchment paper.

In a medium sized bowl, mix together flours, tapioca starch, baking powder, and salt.

Measure shortening/butter into the same bowl, and cut into the dry ingredients using a pastry cutter or fork(s). The idea is to work it in until it's evenly distributed throughout, in very small pieces. Add milk/buttermilk, stir just until dough comes together. Don't over stir or beat it. If dough is too crumbly, add a small amount of extra milk. If the dough is sticky, add a small amount of flour. Pull dough together into a ball, place on a lightly floured work surface. Gently roll dough out to about 3/4 – 1" thick, and cut into rounds with a drinking glass. (I like to use about 3" diameter).

Arrange biscuits on prepared baking sheet. Bake for 12-14 minutes, or until golden brown on top.

Serve hot!

Biscuits and Gravy

Shortly after I moved to the US, I heard of "biscuits and gravy" for the first time. I have no idea if we have it back home or not, but it was the first time I'd ever been exposed to it. We were watching TV, and whatever show it was was demonstrating it. The cook lobbed a big chunk of shortening into the pan for making the gravy, and at that point... I think it was the most disgusting breakfast idea I'd ever even heard of. It didn't even really matter that I later found out that not all biscuit gravy is made like that, the idea of it was gross.

Even without that visual introduction, the idea of anything white being called gravy seemed – and still seems – really OFF to me. Gravy is supposed to be brown! I decided to make biscuits and gravy for my husband, but with a proper brown gravy. In my personal opinion, if you're using flour to thicken anything aside from a delicate white wine sauce, you should make a proper roux. Usually "the darker the better", too!

You see, when it comes to food... browning is flavour. Whether it's a meat, a crust, a cookie... browning your food is adding all kinds of wonderful flavours to it. Why go with a white gravy, when a brown one takes only a few minutes more? I don't get it.

So, rather than just looking at the flour as a thickening agent alone, I look at it as a way to add flavour. When you cook the flour and butter together as a roux, it turns into a rich, toasty, almost nutty flavour – it's the best way to start any gravy, really.

Now, most people recommend cooking your roux over medium or lower heat, and it can take a really long time. If you're just starting out with rouxs, I'd say caution is probably a good idea... but just as an FYI, I usually cook them on high. As long as you're careful, don't stop stirring, and have your liquid pre-measured and ready to go... I find it pretty low risk.

You may find that you need more or less milk than called for here, partially out of personal taste (we like it pretty thick, you may not!), and partially because making a roux isn't really an exact science, when it comes to thickening. As roux cooks and darkens, it loses some of its thickening power. When you first mix the butter and flour together, it will thicken a LOT more liquid than a similiar amount of a really dark brown roux. Play around with it, and see where your preferences take you!

Serves 3-4

1 recipe Baking Powder Biscuits		
Chub sausage of choice	12 oz	375 g
Butter	4 Tbsp	60 ml
White or brown rice flour	4 Tbsp	60 ml
Milk	1.5 cups+	375 ml
Salt and pepper to taste		

Preheat oven for biscuits. While it's heating up, brown the sausage in a fry pan. Remove sausage from pan, set aside. Take note of approximately how much fat you have left in the pan*

Put biscuits in the oven, make the gravy:

Melt butter in that same frying pan. Stir in flour until smooth. Cook over medium or medium-high heat, stirring constantly, until it's as brown as you want it.

Slowly add in about half of the milk, stirring until smooth. Add the rest of the milk, stirring once again until smooth.

Add in the cooked sausage, stir well and bring up to a simmer – the gravy will thicken as it simmers. Add a little more milk if the gravy is too thick for your tastes, then season with salt and pepper to taste.

Keep gravy warm until biscuits come out of the oven. Split warm biscuits in half, smother with gravy.

Enjoy!

* I love using the Papa George's brand of sausage. It's about a million times better than anything else on the market, is perfectly seasoned and flavoured, and has almost no fat in it. We'll use either the regular, hot, or sage flavoured sausage chubs in this recipe. Because this recipe was developed with that particular sausage, you may find yourself wanting to use less butter, if you use a fattier sausage. As an example, if you have about 2 Tbsp of fat left in the pan, decrease the butter by 2 Tbsp. Easy!

Biscuits and Gravy

Paska

When I was growing up, my favourite part of Easter was the Paska bread. My grandmother's neighbor Mary Morin would bake it every year and share it with us. After the egg hunt was over, I knew we'd be going to my grandmother's and this delicious, citrussy bread would be waiting for us. SO GOOD. It's sweet - almost like a cross between a cake and a bread - and she used to bake it in coffee cans. It's traditionally served at Ukrainian Easter celebrations, and I think of it as a breakfast bread.

Even after growing up and moving out, the memories of that bread were so vivid, I asked for the recipe. It's always interesting when you're trying to get a recipe through a game of telephone – especially when the first two passes are through little old ladies! As usual with my family, the recipe came as more of a formula – no instructions - and I adapted it a little (increased the flour, increased the zest, changed lard to butter, ditched the coffee can in favor of decorated style), figured out what the directions should be, etc. The adapted recipe became a hugely popular post on my food blog, and an Easter tradition for my husband and I.

Shortly after finding out that I was allergic to gluten, I had to prepare three batches of that bread for a media appearance. It was killing me - the process, the aromas... and I couldn't have any of it! I decided that I would HAVE to come up with an alternative recipe. The first one was OK, at the time. I used a retail GF flour mixture, and it was more or less edible. The bean flour definitely shone through, though.

This version isn't quite the same as the original, in terms of texture. It's more of a quick bread texture, than the pillowy soft gluten version - but ALL of the flavour is there. I chose to bake it in a bundt pant, to allow for some degree of "decorative" feel to it. There seem to be some wildly different ideas of what Paska entails – many don't have citrus, some have a frosting – but this is based on what I was raised on, and it won't disappoint!

I prefer this bread served warm, either fresh out of the oven or microwaved. Cut into one of your warm loaves, slather with butter, and … don't plan on going anywhere for awhile. It's easy to plow through a ton of this, and it will give you a bread coma. SO WORTH IT. It also makes AMAZING French toast - just put a little vanilla, orange zest, and a splash of OJ in the custard… MMMmmm…

PS: I am glad that I double checked Mary's last name. For some reason, I originally typed "Mallon" instead of "Morin". Mary Mallon. Yes. How's that for a *food* related name screw up? Typhoid Fever is the new Truffle Oil?

Makes 1 Bundt round

Warm water	1/4 cup	50 ml
Granulated sugar	1 tsp	5 ml
2 packets active dry yeast	4 1/2 tsp	22 ml
Light buckwheat flour	1 cup	250 ml
Sorghum flour	1 cup	250 ml
Sweet white rice flour	1 cup	250 ml
Coconut flour	1/2 cup	125 ml
White rice flour	1/2 cup	125 ml
Tapioca starch	1/4 cup	50 ml
Baking powder	2 tsp	10 ml
Baking soda	1/2 tsp	2 ml
Xanthan gum	1 Tbsp	15 ml
Butter, room temperature	1/2 cup	125 ml
Granulated sugar	1 cup	250 ml
Large eggs, beaten	3	3
Juice of 1 lemon and 1 orange		
Zest of 1 lemon and 1 orange		
Salt	1 tsp	5 ml
Scalded milk, cooled	1 cup	250 ml
Pan spray or shortening		

Stir sugar into warm water. Sprinkle yeast on top of sugar water, gently incorporate. Allow to sit for 10-15 minutes, until bubbly. While waiting, whisk together flours, starch, baking powder, baking soda, and xanthan gum. Set aside.

In a stand mixer, cream together butter and sugar until fluffy. Add eggs, continue to cream until well incorporated and fluffy once more.

Add juices, zest, and salt to the mixture, mix until combined. Add scalded milk, continue to mix until well incorporated and smooth. Add 1 cup of the flour mixture, combine well. Add yeast mixture, mix until well incorporated. With mixer on a low setting, slowly add remaining flour mixture - a little at a time. Once all remaining flour has been used up, allow to continue mixing until smooth.

Grease a bundt pan with pan spray or shortening. Transfer dough to prepared pan, cover with plastic wrap, and allow to rise in a warm area for an hour.

Preheat oven to 350F (180 C).

Bake for 10 minutes. Without opening the oven door, lower the heat to 325°F and continue to bake for another 30 minutes. Check for doneness - insert a toothpick or knife into the center of the bread. If it comes out clean, it's done. If not, continue baking until it's fully baked.

Cool Paska for 10-15 minutes (if you can handle the wait), then gently remove turn pan over onto a wire rack or wooden cutting board to continue cooling. Wrap tightly in plastic wrap, eat within a few days.

Paska
45

Appetizers & Sides

Mushroom Turnovers

Mushroom turnovers are one of those things that I'm pretty much expected to bring to certain events. It's kind of weird to think of such a simple thing as being such a signature dish, but people really go nuts for these - myself and my husband included. Generally speaking, I recommend doubling this recipe whenever a group of people is involved - you'd be shocked how fast these disappear!

Makes 30-35 turnovers

White rice flour	3/4 cup	175 ml
Light buckwheat flour	3/4 cup	175 ml
Millet flour	1/2 cup	125 ml
Sweet rice flour	1/4 cup	50 ml
Corn starch	1/4 cup	50 ml
Xanthan	2 tsp	10 ml
1 brick cream cheese	8 oz	250 g
Cold butter	1/2 cup	125 ml
Large egg	1	1
Cold water	1/4 cup	50 ml

Measure flours, corn starch, and xanthan gum into the bowl of your food processor, blitz to combine. Add cream cheese, butter, and egg, blitz a few times until mixture resembles gravel. Stream in cold water as you run the food processor, just long enough to bring it together as a dough.

Remove dough from processor, knead lightly to bring it together as a ball. Wrap in plastic film, chill for 1 hour.

Baby bella mushroom slices	1 lb	500 g
Medium onion	1	1
Garlic cloves, pressed	3	3
Olive oil	2 Tbsp	30 ml
Fresh thyme, finely chopped	4 tsp	20 ml
Sea salt	1 tsp	5 ml
Sour cream	1/2 cup	125 ml
Large egg	1	1
Water	1 tsp	5 ml

In food processor (or by hand, ew) chop mushrooms, onion, and garlic together, until mushrooms and onions are small, fairly uniform sized bits. Place mushrom mixture in frying pan with olive oil, and cook down until mushrooms are very soft – almost mushy. Add thyme and sea salt, remove from heat, cool to room temperature. Once mushrom mixture has cooled, strain off any excess liquid and stir in the sour cream. Chill until use.

Preheat oven to 450F (230 C). Line 2 baking sheets with parchment paper.

Roll chilled dough out to about 1/4" thick. Use a large glass or cookie cutter (about 3-4" in diameter) to cut out rounds.

Put a rounded tsp or two of filling in the center of each round. Whisk the egg and water in a mug, brush a small amount along ½ the edge of each round. Using the egg mix like a glue, fold each round in half to enclose the mushroom filling. Press firmly around the edges to seal completely, arrange turnovers onto a prepared baking sheet.

Brush the tops of turnovers with egg wash, then pierce each with a fork a few times. Bake for 12-15 minutes, until golden.

Serve hot or cold.

Mushroom Turnovers

Pao de Queijo

If you've ever been to a Brazilian "Churrasqueira" type restaurant, you may recognize these little balls of awesome - they're addictive little buns that are inherently gluten-free.

Soft and satisfying, they make a good snack - you may find yourself going through a dozen in a sitting, before you even realize it! They're also very easy to make - the batter whips up in a blender, and they're poured into mini muffin tins to bake!

Makes about 24 mini buns

Large eggs	2	2
Olive oil	1/2 cup	125 ml
Milk	1 cup	250 ml
Tapioca starch	2 1/4 cup	550 ml
Shredded cheese (I like Asiago)	3/4 cup	175 ml
Salt	1 1/2 tsp	7 ml
Pan spray		

Preheat oven to 400 F (200 C). Prepare a mini muffin pan with pan spray.

Combine all ingredients in a blender, blitz until well blended and smooth. Divide batter between 24 mini muffin cavities. Bake for 15-20 minutes, until puffy and golden brown.

Pao de Queijo

Gougères

Somewhat like Pao de Queijo, but a little more work. Instead of a chewy texture, these are a pastry - picture a cheesy cream puff, without the cream. These can be sliced in half to make mini sandwich style hors d'ouevres, filled with cheese, or eaten plain. (My husband says he actually prefers paos because they fit on his fingers, "like 'Bugles'!")

Makes about 30

Milk	1 cup	250 ml
Butter	1/4 cup	50 ml
Salt	1/2 tsp	2 ml
Sweet rice flour	1/3 cup	75 ml
White rice flour	1/3 cup	75 ml
Millet flour	1/3 cup	75 ml
Cayenne pepper	1/4 tsp	1 ml
Mustard powder	1/2 tsp	2 ml
Xanthan gum	1 tsp	5 ml
Baking powder	1/2 tsp	2 ml
Large eggs	3	3
Large egg whites	2	2
Grated Swiss cheese	1 cup	250 ml

Preheat oven to 400 F (200 C). Line a baking sheet with parchment paper or a nonstick baking sheet. It's very important to not grease the pan - it will cause the pastries to flatten!

Combine milk, butter and salt in a medium sauce pan, heat to a boil. In a separate bowl, combine flours, cayenne, mustard powder, xanthan gum, and baking powder. Remove from heat, add flour mixture, stirring until well incorporated.

Reduce heat to medium, return saucepan to stove top. Cook for another minute or so, until the dough comes together, leaving the sides of the pan. Transfer dough to the bowl of your stand mixer. Using the paddle attachment, beat the dough for a minute or so to allow it to cool slightly.

Meanwhile, beat together eggs and egg whites in a small bowl. With the mixer set to medium, add egg mixture to dough a little at a time, allowing eggs to fully incorporate into the dough before adding more. It may look like a separating mess, but I promise it will come together! Once all of the eggs have been added and the dough is once again smooth, add cheese and continue beating ti melt and distribute.

Once the dough is smooth and shiny, it's ready to pipe! It'll be soft and a bit sticky, but more or less be able to hold its shape.

Line a baking sheet with parchment. Using spoons or a pastry bags, make walnut-sized mounds of batter, leaving 2" of space between each. Use a moistened finger to pat down any peaks of dough that may form as you finish piping each.

Bake for 12 minutes, then - WITHOUT opening the oven door - turn the temperature down to 350 F (180 C) and bake for another 25 minutes. Crack the oven door open a few inches, turn the heat off, and allow the puffs to cool in the oven for 30 minutes. This step allows the insides to dry out, providing a stronger structure to prevent collapse.

Gougères

Quick Falafel Patties

As with many ethnic recipes – well, recipes in general, I suppose – there is a traditional way to do it, and there are the nontraditional ways to do it. Generally speaking, non traditional versions usually act as a workaround to some unwieldly aspect of the original – a hard to come by ingredient, a specialty piece of equipment, etc. In some cases, it's simply a matter of saving time.

Such is the case with my quick version of falafel. Traditionally, these are made from dried chick peas – soaked overnight and then ground down for the batter, and then deep fried. In this version, we strain canned chickpeas, and use the addition of garbanzo/fava flour to prevent them from falling apart. The use of bean flour – rather than a wheat flour – makes these not gluten-free, but also full of flavour!

Small onion, peeled and chopped	1	1
Garlic cloves, pressed	1-2	1-2
Can garbanzo beans, drained well	15 oz	500 g
Large egg	1	1
Garbanzo/fava flour	1/4 cup	50 ml
Coriander	1 tsp	5 ml
Salt	1 tsp	5 ml
Baking powder	1 tsp	5 ml
Pepper	1/2 tsp	2 ml
Cayenne pepper	pinch	pinch
Lemon juice	1 tsp	5 ml
Olive oil	1 Tbsp	15 ml

Process onion, garlic, and half of the beans till smooth. Add remaining ingredients (aside from remaining beans and olive oil), process till smooth. Add remaining beans, process till new beans are small but chunky.

Heat olive oil in a nonstick pan, swirl to coat well. Use a large Tablespoon, 1/4 cup measure, or cookie scoop to drop balls of batter into fry pan, carefully flatten them a bit. Fry for a couple minutes on the first side, flipping when golden brown. Fry on other side until also golden brown.

Serve hot, with tahini or cucumber dill dip.

Cucumber Dill Dip

Plain Greek yogurt	1 cup	250 ml
Grated seedless cucumber	1 cup	250 ml
Fresh dill, chopped	1/4 cup	50 ml
Garlic cloves, pressed	2	2 ml
Salt and pepper		

Combine yogurt, cucumber, dill, and garlic. Season with salt and pepper to taste

Quick Falafel Patties

Cornbread

Cornbread seems like such a basic food item, but it takes customization beautifully. I love using roasted jalapenos in mine, and of course you can always throw in a handful or two of sharp cheddar cheese. Increase the sugar a bit for a sweeter cornbread (up to about 1/2 cup), or leave it as-is for savoury. Use yellow, white, blue, or red cornmeal.. or marble a couple of colours together!

Cornmeal*	2 cups	500 ml
Light buckwheat flour	1/2 cup	125 ml
Masa flour	1/4 cup	50 ml
Sorghum flour	1/2 cup	125 ml
Tapioca starch	1/3 cup	75 ml
Baking powder	2 tsp	10 ml
Baking soda	1/2 tsp	2 ml
Salt	2 tsp	10 ml
Large eggs	2	2
Granulated sugar	2 Tbsp	30 ml
Sour cream	3/4 cup	175 ml
Milk	1 1/2 cups	375 ml

Preheat oven to 350 F (180 C) , spray a 9" x 12" baking pan with pan spray.

In a large mixing bowl, combine cornmeal, flours, tapioca starch, baking powder, baking soda, and salt.

In a separate mixing bowl, whisk eggs, sugar and sour cream together until smooth. Slowly add milk and chicken broth, whisking until everything is well combined. Pour into the dry ingredients, stir just until everything is combined.

Scoop batters into the pan. Bake for 30-35 minutes, or until knife inserted into the center comes out clean.

* Cornmeal comes in several varieties, with some being more available than others. While yellow is most popular for cornbread, and white is readily available alongside yellow... consider trying red (pink) or blue. Red cornmeal tends to be even sweeter than regular yellow cornmeal, and produces a lovely pink cornbread. Blue cornmeal tends to have a roasty, earthy, flavour. If you can't find them in your local store, it's worth it to order them online!

What do you do when you have two new cornmeals to play with, and can't decide where to start? Simple, you marble them together!

To make marbled cornbread, do a batch of the recipe as described, but leave out the cornmeal. Divide the batter equally between 2 mixing bowls. Add 1 cup of one cornmeal to one bowl, and 1 cup of another cornmeal to the second bowl, stirring each well to combine.

Scoop batters into the pan, randomly alternating colours throughout. To marble the batters, use a butter knife, held straight up-and-down. Starting at one side of the pan, run the knife through the batter in a long zig zag motion – hitting both the "top" and "bottom" of the pan, from your view – all the way to the other side. Then, turn the pan 90 degrees, and repeat.

Not only is this cornbread pretty, the contrast in colours, tastes, and texture is really interesting, a unique cornbread.

Roasted Jalapeno: Cut 2-3 jalapeños in half, removing ribs and seeds if you prefer a milder bread. Brush peppers with olive oil. Grill or broil until as "done" as you like (I prefer some dark grill marks but not an overall char). Remove from heat, allow to cool. Chop the peppers, and mix into batter with the wet ingredients

.

Roasted Jalapeno Cornbread

Corn Dogs

Corn dogs are something that really don't need to be full of wheat flour, but tend to be anyway. Personally, I prefer the flavour and texture that comes from using masa - corn flour - instead of wheat flour. This is the same flour used to make tamales, and gives it a more unadulterated corn flavour.

Makes 8 corn dogs

Vegetable Oil for deep frying		
Gluten free beef hot dogs	8	8
Masa, plus extra for dusting	1 cup	250 ml
White rice flour	3/4 cup	175 ml
Yellow corn meal	1/4 cup	50 ml
Tapioca starch	1 Tbsp	15 ml
Xanthan gum	1 tsp	5 ml
Salt	1 tsp	5 ml
Granulated sugar	2 Tbsp	30 ml
Baking powder	2 tsp	10 ml
Baking soda	1/2 tsp	2 ml
Large eggs	2	2
Buttermilk	2 cup	500 ml
Butter, melted	1/4 cup	50 ml
Optional:		
Cayenne pepper	1/4 tsp	50 ml
Mustard powder	1/2 tsp	2 ml
Onion powder	1/4 tsp	1 ml
Corn dog skewers	8	8

Heat oil 375 F (190 C). You can use a deep fryer, or a heavy pan. If not using a deep fryer, use a deep, heavy pot, filled to at least 3" deep.

Dry the hotdogs off with napkins WELL. Dust with a little masa flour, set aside

Combine all dry ingredients - including seasonings, if using - whisking to combine. In a separate bowl, whisk eggs, buttermilk, and melted butter together. Combine wet and dry ingredients, mixing until well combined and relatively smooth. Transfer batter to a tall glass, cover with plastic film, allow to sit for 10 minutes.

If using skewers, stick them into hotdogs, making sure they go in to about halfway up the length of the hotdog.

Gently dip hotdogs in the batter one at a time, slowly removing from the batter and allowing excess to drip off. Carefully transfer dipped hot dogs to heated oil. Fry a few at a time - turning every few minutes - until golden brown.

Corn Dogs

Hush Puppies

Much like with corn dogs, I find the use of wheat flour in hush puppies to be unnecessary, and definitely prefer the use of masa.

This makes a moderately sweet batch of hush puppies, and the sugar can be adjusted to your personal taste. Do you like cornbread to be really sweet? Bump it up to 1/2 cup of sugar. Prefer a cornbread that's only slightly sweet? Decrease the sugar down to a Tablespoon or two!

Oil for deep frying		
Yellow corn meal	1 cup	250 ml
White rice flour	1/2 cup	125 ml
Masa flour	1/2 cup	125 ml
Tapioca starch	1 Tbsp	15 ml
Xanthan gum	1 tsp	5 ml
Salt	1 tsp	5 ml
Granulated sugar	1/3 cup	75 ml
Baking powder	2 tsp	10 ml
Baking soda	1/2 tsp	2 ml
Large eggs	2	2
Buttermilk	2 cups	500 ml
Butter, melted	1/4 cup	50 ml
Medium onion, finely chopped	1	1

Heat oil 375F (190 C)

Combine all dry ingredients, whisking to combine. In a separate bowl, whisk eggs, buttermilk, melted butter, and chopped onion together.

Combine wet and dry ingredients, mixing until well combined and relatively smooth. Cover with plastic film, allow to sit for 10 minutes.

Gently drop rounded teaspoons of batter into the heated oil. Fry in small batches - allowing oil to come back up to temperature between each batch - until golden brown.

Hush Puppies
59

Pakora

I love Pakora. Chicken, veggie, paneer... doesn't matter. Give me a plate of it, and a big helping of cilantro-mint chutney, and I'm a happy camper.

Unfortunately, most Indian restaurants either cut their batter with wheat flour, or cross-contaminate it with other flour items. Not worth the risk... so I started making pakora at home. All the flavour, none of the risk... and not having to deal with noisy restaurants? Score!

Chicken and Paneer Pakora

This makes enough batter for 3-4 large boneless chicken breasts, or 2 bricks of paneer. Well, or ~2 chicken breasts and 1 brick of paneer - variety is always good!

Oil, for deep frying		
garbanzo (chickpea) flour	1 1/4 cups	300 ml
White rice flour	1/4 cup	50 ml
Hot curry powder	1 1/2 tsp	7 ml
Coriander powder	1/2 tsp	2 ml
Salt	1 tsp	5 ml
Baking powder	1/4 tsp	1 ml
Finely chopped fresh cilantro	2 Tbsp	30 ml
Water	1 cup	250 ml
Additional garbanzo flour	1/4 cup	50 ml

Start heating your oil to 375F (190 C) – you'll want at least 2-3" of oil in your pot or deep fryer.

In a large bowl, combine flours, spices, salt, baking powder, and cilantro. Add water, stir well to form a thick batter. All batter to sit for 5 minutes or so, to soften the bean flour.

For Chicken Pakora:

Slice your chicken breasts into fingers, toss with additional garbanzo flour, then dredge in the batter.

Carefully transfer a few battered chicken fingers to the preheated oil. Fry for a few minutes on each side, until golden brown and cooked through. Use a slotted metal spoon to transfer fried chicken to paper towels.

Serve hot, with cilantro-mint chutney. (Page 63)

For Paneer Pakora:

Slice your paneer into long fingers about 1" x 1", by however wide your paneer bricks are. Toss cheese sticks with additional garbanzo flour, then dredge in the batter.

Carefully transfer a few battered sticks of paneer to the preheated oil. Fry for a few minutes on each side, until golden brown. Use a slotted metal spoon to transfer fried paneer to paper towels.

Serve hot, with cilantro-mint chutney. (Page 63)

Mixed Pakoras

Mixed Vegetable Pakora

Mixed veggie pakora may be my favourite type of pakora. I love the complex flavours, all of the colour, the variety of textures. It's also a great way to use up stray vegetables in your fridge – Root vegetables like carrots, parsnips, and sweet potatoes, cruciferous veggies like broccoli, cauliflower, etc .. basically anything that's tasty and kind of sturdy. (Ie: don't use tomatoes!). For this recipe, I decided to specify amounts – I'd created this to have a great balance in flavours, colour, and texture.

Like many of my recipes, this works up quickly and easily, producing a highly addictive end product. Expect a "pakora coma" after snarfing these babies!

Vegetable oil for deep frying		
Garbanzo flour	1 1/4 cups	300 ml
White rice flour	1/4 cup	50 ml
Salt	2 tsp	10 ml
Hot curry powder	1 1/2 tsp	7 ml
Cumin	1 tsp	5 ml
Baking powder	1/4 tsp	2 ml
Water	1 cup	250 ml
Finely chopped broccoli	1 cup	250 ml
Finely chopped yam / sweet potato	1 cup	250 ml
Finely chopped zucchini	1 cup	250 ml
Finely chopped onion	1 cup	250 ml
Jalapenos, finely chopped	1-2	1-2
Fresh cilantro, chopped	1/2 cup	125 ml

Start heating your vegetable oil to 375F (190 C) – you'll want at least 2-3" of oil in your pot or deep fryer.

In a large bowl, combine flours, salt, spices, and baking powder. Add water, stir well to form a thick batter. All batter to sit for 5 minutes or so, to soften the bean flour.

Mix in remaining ingredients, making sure that everything is evenly coated with the batter.

Use an ice cream scoop or two spoons to carefully scoop small amounts (1/4 cup or less) of batter into the preheated oil. Fry for a few minutes on each side, until patties are golden brown. Use a slotted metal spoon to transfer cooked patties to paper towels.

Serve hot, with cilantro-mint chutney (Page 63)

Mixed Veggie Pakora

Cilantro-Mint Chutney

Cilantro Mint Chutney is a popular condiment in Indian cooking, and pairs so perfectly with a plateful of Pakora.

Fresh cilantro	2 bunches	2 bunches
fresh mint leaves	2 bunches	2 bunches
Jalapeno, chopped	1	1
Juice of 1/2 large lime		
Salt	1/2 tsp	2 ml
Cumin	1 tsp	5 ml
Granulated sugar	1 tsp	5 ml

Measure everything but the cilantro into a food processor, pulse into finely chopped – almost a paste. Add a handful of cilantro, pulse til combined. Add the rest of the cilantro, pulse until well chopped and combined. Cover and refrigerate until use.

Dosa / "Fauxsa"

They say "Necessity is the mother of invention", and I've never found that to be as true, as it has been since being diagnosed with gluten allergies. It's amazing what you can come up with, when someone takes your bread away! Maybe "Desperation" is the father of invention?

Anyway. I was enjoying a dosa at a local Indian restaurant last year, lustfully eyeing my husband's naan… when it hit me. What if I used the ingredients and basic concept of dosa (a paper thin, crispy Indian crepe), but made it much thicker, to be a makeshift substitute for naan?

… and so I did. It worked beautifully! I give you… "Fauxsa", as my husband dubbed it that first day. This tastes great and satisfies completely. It's sturdy enough to use as a dip for Indian foods, and goes ridiculously well with melted curry butter.

Stickler for tradition? Add a little more water and follow directions for cooking crepes (Page 33), to make an actual Dosa!

Dry long grain white rice	2 cups	500 ml
Dry red lentils	1/2 cup	125 ml
Dry yellow split peas	1/2 cup	125 ml
Mustard seeds	1 tsp	5 ml
Yeast	1/4 tsp	1 ml
Salt	1/2 tsp	2 ml

In a large bowl, mix together rice, lentils, split peas, and mustard seeds. Cover completely with hot water, to about 1" above the rice mixture level. Allow to soak at room temperature overnight.

In the morning, strain mixture, reserving about 1 cup of the rice water. Place strained rice and beans mixture into a food processor with about 1/4 cup of the reserved rice water, puree for about 5 minutes, or until very, VERY smooth.

Transfer rice batter to a large bowl, stir in yeast and salt. Add enough of the rice water (if needed) to make a very thick batter, about the consistency of THICK pancake batter.

Cover bowl with a clean tea towel, allow to ferment in a warm place for a few hours. Once you've fermented the mixture, give it a good stir – some separation will have occurred. (Note: it'll smell awful. That's ok – the finished product does not!)

Heat up a nonstick fry pan (Medium heat), spray with a little pan spray. Pour about 1 cup of rice batter into the middle of the pan, swirling it out to make a "pancake" about 6-8" across. Allow to cook for a few minutes, until the bottom is set and browning, with air bubbles popping on the top. Carefully flip, continuing to cook on the other side. Cook until batter is completely cooked, all the way through. Serve hot.

"Fauxsa"

Pita

Sometimes, you can achieve the goal you're looking for, but still be surprised by an added "bonus". Such was the case with these pitas. The dough was a dream to work with - great texture, easy to roll, etc. It baked up to a lovely golden brown. It looked right, it handled right, it held up to making a sandwich. As my husband and I bit into our pita sandwiches for the first time, we both realized that this pita tasted extremely familiar to us. Not like store bought pita bread, more like... yes, this tasted exactly like Jimmy John's bread! I don't know if they actually use any alternate flours in their bread to achieve that flavour, but hey - as a former JJ addict, I'll take it!

Makes about 5 Pitas

Warm water	1/2 cup	125 ml
Granulated sugar	1 tsp	5 ml
1 packet instant yeast	2 1/4 tsp	11 ml
Brown rice flour	1 cup	250 ml
Amaranth flour	1/2 cup	125 ml
Millet flour	1/2 cup	125 ml
Sorghum flour	1/2 cup	125 ml
Corn starch	1/2 cup	125 ml
Tapioca starch	1/4 cup	50 ml
Xanthan gum	2 tsp	10 ml
Salt	1 1/2 tsp	7 ml
Large egg	1	1
Warm milk	1 cup	250 ml
Olive oil	2 Tbsp	30 ml

Combine warm water with sugar, stirring until sugar is almost dissolved. Add yeast, stirring until incorporated. Cover bowl with plastic wrap. Set aside in a warm place for 10 minutes, or until foamy.

In a very large mixing bowl (stand mixer if you have it!), combine flours, starches, xanthan gum and salt, whisking until well combined. Whisk egg into yeast mixture, add to the dry ingredients and stir until well combined. Slowly add milk , mixing well to combine.

Pour olive oil into a large clean bowl, swirl to coat the bottom and sides of the bowl. Transfer dough to oiled bowl, flip to coat in oil. Loosely cover with plastic wrap, allow to rise in a warm place for an hour or two.

Preheat oven to 450 F (230 C), line two cookie sheets with parchment paper

Divide dough into 5 equal sized portions. Roll into rounds about 6-8" across. Transfer a couple pita rounds to each cookie sheet, spaced apart. Bake for 6-7 minutes, until puffy and golden. Flip over and bake for 2-3 more minutes. Repeat for all remaining disks. Serve right away (Cut in half, then slit open with a sharp knife to make pockets!), or store in plastic baggies for up to a few days (fresh), or freeze for up to 3 weeks.

Pita

Gyoza

Gyoza

Gyoza... what is there to say about gyoza? Done right, these are supremely addictive. Yes, they're supposed to be an appetizer, usually served 3-5 pieces per person... but I've lost count of how many times we've made a meal of them. (No, I'm not admitting to how many constitute a "meal", either!). They're ingredient-intensive and a bit of work, but SO worth it!

I love gyoza with a ton of flavour, so I developed this recipe with that in mind. The filling can be made a day ahead, just keep it well chilled. Finished gyoza can be frozen before frying/steaming - just be sure to allow them to thaw completely before cooking.

Makes about 40

Raw shrimp	1/2 lb	250 g
Napa cabbage, finely shredded	1/2	1/2
Salt	1 tsp	5 ml
Ground pork	1 1/2 lbs	750 g
Grated ginger	1-2 Tbsp	15-30 ml
Garlic cloves, pressed or minced	5	5
Green onions, finely chopped	2	2
Sesame oil	1-2 Tbsp	15-30 ml
Crushed chilies	1 tsp	5 ml
Granulated sugar	1/2 tsp	2 ml

Thaw (if applicable), peel, devein, and finely chop the shrimp, set aside. In a large mixing bowl, combine cabbage and salt, stirring to evenly distribute the salt. Allow to sit for 10-15 minutes - this will draw the moisture out of the cabbage.

Once time is up, squeeze as much water out of the cabbage as you can, discarding the water. Place the squeezed cabbage back into the mixing bowl.

Add all remaining ingredients - aside from the wrappers and oil - to the bowl, and mix thoroughly. I like to use my hands for this - does a much better job of distributing everything than any mixing spoon will! Cover and chill until ready to use.

Gyoza Wrappers

Sorghum flour	1 cup	250 ml
Tapioca starch	2/3 cup	150 ml
Sweet rice flour	1/3 cup	75 ml
Potato starch, plus extra for rolling	1/3 cup	75 ml
Corn starch	1/3 cup	75 ml
Salt	1/2 tsp	2 ml
Xanthan	2 tsp	10 ml
Sour cream	1 cup	250 ml
Large eggs	2	2
Warm milk	1/3 cup	75 ml

Measure all dry ingredients into the bowl of your food processor, blitz to combine. Add sour cream, and eggs, blitz a few times until mixture resembles gravel. Stream in milk as you run the food processor, just long enough to bring it together as a dough.

Remove dough from processor, knead lightly to bring it together as a ball. Wrap dough in plastic film, allow to sit on counter for 1 hour.

Once time is up, knead dough a few times. It should be soft and easy to work, but not sticky.

Sprinkle your work surface with potato starch, roll your dough out very thin - less than 1/8" thick. (Think "wonton wrapper" thickness). Use a cookie cutter or glass to cut into 3" round circles.

To assemble:

Gyoza filling	1 batch	1 batch
Gyoza wrappers	1 batch	1 batch
Vegetable, olive, or sesame oil	2 Tbsp	30 ml

Roll filling into tight 1" balls, placing one in the middle of each wrapper.

Use a finger/pastry brush dipped in water to moisten the edges of each wrapper. Fold the wrapper over the filling, creating a half circle. As you do this, try to push out as much of the air from the inside as possible - excess air can cause them to burst.

Use a dumpling press to seal and crimp the edges, or pleat the edges by hand.

Heat up the 2 Tbsp vegetable, olive, or sesame oil in a frying pan (I prefer to use nonstick for this), and arrange a single layer of gyoza in the pan - not touching each other. Cook until bottom side is nicely browned.

Once the bottom is browned to your liking, pour 1/3 cup of warm water into the pan, and quickly cover with a lid. Cook for 2-3 minutes without removing the lid.

After 2-3 minutes, remove the lid and allow gyoza to continue cooking until all of the water has cooked off. Serve hot, with gyoza sauce

Gyoza Sauce

Gluten-free soy sauce	1/2 cup	125 ml
Rice vinegar	1/4 cup	50 ml
Crushed chilies	1 tsp	2 ml

Stir ingredients together, refrigerate til serving.

Egg Rolls

Egg rolls were one of the first things I really missed when having to go gluten-free. While it would be really nice to be able to order safe ones when out, these are easy enough to make that you can make them whenever the mood strikes!

Makes about 20

Shredded Napa cabbage	2 cups	500 ml
Salt	1/2 tsp	2 ml
Ground pork	1 1/2 lbs	750 g
Small carrot, grated	1/2	1/2
Grated ginger	1 Tbsp	15 ml
Garlic cloves, pressed or minced	3	3
Green onion, finely chopped	1	1
Sesame oil	1-2 Tbsp	15- 30 ml
Egg roll wrappers	1 batch	1 batch
Oil for frying		

In a large mixing bowl, combine cabbage and salt, stirring to evenly distribute the salt. Allow to sit for 10-15 minutes - this will draw the moisture out of the cabbage.

While you wait for the cabbage, brown the ground pork. When it's almost completely cooked, add the carrots and continue to cook until they start to soften slightly. Drain off fat, allow to cool.

Once time is up, squeeze as much water out of the cabbage as you can, discarding the water. Place the squeezed cabbage back into the mixing bowl. Add drained pork and all remaining ingredients - aside from the wrappers and oil - to the bowl, and mix thouroughly. I like to use my hands for this - does a much better job of distributing everything than any mixing spoon will!

Cover and chill until ready to use.

Egg Roll Wrappers:

Sorghum flour	1 cup	250 ml
Tapioca starch	2/3 cup	150 ml
Sweet rice flour	1/3 cup	75 ml
Potato starch, plus extra for rolling	1/3 cup	75 ml
Corn starch	1/3 cup	75 ml
Salt	1/2 tsp	2 ml
Xanthan gum	2 tsp	10 ml
Sour cream	1 cup	250 ml
Large eggs	2	2
Warm milk	1/3 cup	75 ml

Measure all dry ingredients into the bowl of your food processor, blitz to combine. Add sour cream, and eggs, blitz a few times until mixture resembles gravel. Stream in milk as you run the food processor, just long enough to bring it together as a dough.

Remove dough from processor, knead lightly to bring it together as a ball. Wrap dough in plastic film, allow to sit on counter for 1 hour. Once time is up, knead dough a few times. It should be soft and easy to work, but not sticky.

Sprinkle your work surface with potato starch, roll your dough out very thin - less than 1/8" thick. (Think "wonton wrapper" thickness). Use a cookie cutter or glass to cut into 3" round circles.

Heat oil up to 375F (190 C) in a deep fryer or heavy pot.

Use a finger/pastry brush dipped in water to moisten the edges of each wrapper. Place about 1/4 cup of filling in a diagonal line across the middle of each wrapper , avoiding about 1" dough at the two side corners it's lined up between. Fold one of the other two corners (let's call them top/bottom corners) over the line of filling, gently pressing to compress the filling. (Too much air will cause the egg rolls to break open when cooking. Fold in the two side corners, taking care to once again not allow excess air in between the layers. Roll the whole thing tightly towards the remaining corner.

Fry egg rolls in small batches, turning every few minutes, until they are golden brown.
Serve hot, with sweet and sour sauce!

Sweet and Sour Sauce
Makes 1 cup

Shredded onion	1/2 cup	120 ml
Grated ginger	1 tsp	5 ml
Sesame oil	1 tsp	5 ml
Garlic cloves, pressed	2	2
Cornstarch	2 tsp	10 ml
Rice vinegar	1/4 cup	50 ml
Orange or pineapple juice	1/2 cup	125 ml
Ketchup	1/4 cup	50 ml
Honey	2 Tbsp	30 ml
Gluten-free soy sauce	2 tsp	10 ml
Sriracha	1 tsp+	5 ml+

In a small saucepan, combine onion, ginger, and olive oil. Cook over medium heat until onions soften and become translucent. In separate bowl, whisk together cornstarch and rice vinegar until smooth. Add juice, continue whisking until once again smooth.

Add cornstarch mixture to pot, alone with remaining ingredients. Bring to a boil, reduce heat and simmer for 3 minutes. Cool to room temperature, then chill until use.

Egg Rolls

Jalapeno Poppers

These are the ultimate jalapeno poppers! Rather than going with the traditional cream cheese filling, these are filled with a mixture of cream and cheddar cheeses, and BACON. Bacon really does make everything better. From there, they're dipped in a flavourful bean batter than cooks up light and fluffy - truly amazing.

Makes 24 poppers (1/2 jalapeno each)

Cream cheese, softened	8 oz	250 g
Cheddar cheese, finely shredded*	1 cup	250 ml
Strips bacon, cooked and crumbled	3-4	3-4
Jalapenos	12	12
Garbanzo (chickpea) flour	2 cups	500 ml
Sorghum flour	2 cups	500 ml
White rice flour	1/2 cup	125 ml
Salt	2 tsp	10 ml
Baking powder	1/2 tsp	2 ml
Cold gluten-free beer (or cold water)	2 cups	500 ml
Vegetable oil, for frying		
Cornstarch	1 cup	250 ml

Cream together cream cheese and cheddar cheese until well combined and relatively smooth, gently fold in bacon. Cover with plastic wrap and chill for at least 1 hour.

Wearing gloves, slice jalapenos in half and remove the seeds. For a more mild popper, remove the rib membrane as well. We like our peppers a bit crunchier, so we use them straight. You can also blanch them by dipping them in boiling water for a minute, and plunging into cold water. Let them dry off fully before stuffing them.

Roll chilled stuffing mixture into about 1" balls, gently stuff into jalapeno halves, pressing firmly. For larger jalapenos, you may need to add more filling. Smooth filling with your finger, chill while working on the batter.

In a large bowl, combine flours, salt, and baking powder. Add beer or water, stir well to form a thick batter. All batter to sit for 5 minutes or so, to soften the bean flour.

Heat oil 375 F (190 C). You can use a deep fryer, or a heavy pan. If not using a deep fryer, use a deep, heavy pot, filled to at least 3" deep.

Gently dredge chilled poppers in cornstarch and knock excess off. Dip dredged poppers in batter, and carefully transfer to preheated oil, cooking in small batches. Fry for about 3 minutes at 375, or until golden brown. Transfer to baking sheet lined with paper towels, to absorb some of the extra oil. Serve hot, with sour cream or ranch dressing as a dip.

* Can also use Monterey jack

Jalapeno Poppers

Brie en Croûte with Prosciutto, Honey Pear Sauce, and Figs

Brie en Croûte with Prosciutto, Honey Pear Sauce, and Figs

If you've never had fresh figs, it may be a bit difficult to picture how this will taste. Unlike their dried counterparts, fresh figs have a dainty, almost floral taste to them. The taste and texture of the fresh figs pairs perfectly with the saltiness of the prosciutto, the creaminess of the cheese, sweetness of the pear-honey sauce, and the crunch from the pistachios.

This makes a very elegant and impressive appetizer OR dessert course!

Light buckwheat flour	1/2 cup	125 ml
White rice flour	1/4 cup	50 ml
Millet flour	1/4 cup	50 ml
Sweet rice flour	1/4 cup	50 ml
Xanthan gum	1 tsp	5 ml
Cream cheese	4 oz	125 g
Cold butter	1/4 cup	50 ml
Large egg	1	1
Cold water	2 Tbsp	30 ml

Measure flours, corn starch, and xanthan gum into the bowl of your food processor, blitz to combine. Add cream cheese, butter, and egg, blitz a few times until mixture resembles gravel. Stream in cold water as you run the food processor, just long enough to bring it together as a dough.

Remove dough from processor, knead lightly to bring it together as a ball. Wrap in plastic film, chill for 1 hour.

Small wheel of brie	1	1
Slices prosciutto	4	4
Large egg	1	1
Water	1 Tbsp	15 ml

Honey Sauce:

Pear juice or pear nectar	2/3 cup	150 ml
Honey	2 Tbsp	30 ml
Lemon juice	1 tsp	5 ml

Black mission figs, sliced	2	2
Finely chopped pistachios	2 Tbsp	30 ml

Preheat oven to 400 F (200 C), line baking sheet with parchment paper

Roll out pastry dough to about 12" diameter. Carefully cut the rind off the brie, if desired. Wrap brie in prosciutto, place in the middle of the pastry round. Pull up all edges of the pastry, to full enclose the brie in a little pouch.

Whisk together egg and water, Lightly brush entire pastry with egg wash. Bake for 30-35 minutes, or until golden brown.

While brie is baking, make the honey sauce: Whisk together juices and honey in a small saucepan. Bring JUST to a boil, turn heat down to low, and simmer for 30 minutes.

As soon as brie is finished baking, transfer to serving plate. Arrange sliced figs on top, drizzle generously with honey pear sauce. Sprinkle with pistachios, serve immediately!

When figs aren't in season, I like to do my Prosciutto Brie en Croûte topped with a quick, savoury pear jam.

Quick Pear Jam:

Olive oil	1 Tbsp	15 ml
Butter	1 Tbsp	15 ml
Sweet onion, thinly sliced	1	1
Garlic cloves, pressed or minced	3	3
Anjou pears, cut into 1" pieces	3	3
Granulated sugar	1/2 cup	125 ml
Dry white wine	1/2 cup	125 ml
Salt, to taste		

Combine olive oil, butter, onion, garlic, and pears. Cook over medium heat until onions start to soften a little. Stir in sugar, cook for about 30 minutes, stirring frequently. Serve over freshly baked brie.

Brie en Croûte with Quick Pear Jam

Onion Blossom

Also called a "Blooming Onion", these are a hit at some chain restaurants... but can be made at home relatively easily! They're deliciously addictive, and will make you want to snarf the whole thing... which probably isn't the best idea. Be sure to have someone to share with!

For a fun alternative and unique flavour, use 1/4 cup corn starch, 1/4 cup rice flour, 1/2 cup mesquite flour

Large sweet onion	1	1

Starch mix:

Corn starch	1/2 cup	125 ml
Salt	1/2 tsp	2 ml
Paprika	1 tsp	5 ml

Batter:

Corn starch	1/2 cup	125 ml
White rice flour	1/2 cup	125 ml
Salt	1 1/2 tsp	7 ml
Cayenne	1 1/2 tsp	7 ml
Paprika	1 tsp	5 ml
Mustard powder	1 tsp	5 ml
Pepper	3/4 tsp	3 ml
Oregano	1/2 tsp	2 ml
Thyme	1/4 tsp	1 ml
Cumin powder	pinch	pinch
Large eggs	2	2
Milk	1/2 cup +	125 ml +

Heat vegetable oil to 375F (190 C). You can use a deep fryer, or a heavy pan. If not using a deep fryer, use a deep, heavy pot, filled to at least 4" deep.

Slice about 1" off the pointy end of the onion, and peel it. Place it cut side down on your work surface, and - being careful to slice about halfway through the width of the onion - make about 16 vertical cuts, starting about 1/2" from the top of the onion.

Flip onion over, gently separate the "petals", and carefully remove the very center of the onion, creating about 1/2" diameter empty core. Set aside.

Whisk together starch mix ingredients. Use a large plastic bag, place onion and starch mix in, and gently shake to fully coat. Discard remaining starch mix. Allow onion to sit for ten minutes, as you prepare the batter:

Whisk together all dry ingredients until well combined. Add eggs and milk, whisk until smooth. Allow to sit for 10 minutes.

Place onion in mixing bowl, cut side up. Separate petals as best you can, gently pour batter over the onion. Swirl bowl around to coat onion thoroughly.

Carefully place onion in deep fryer, cut side down. Fry for 5 minutes, then carefully flip over and fry for another 5 minutes or so, until golden brown. Transfer to plate lined with paper towels, blot any excess grease before carefully transferring to serving plate.

Serve hot, with your choice of dipping sauce:

Traditional: 1/4 cup (50 ml) sour cream, 1/4 cup (50 ml) mayo, 2+ Tbsp (30+ ml) horseradish (to taste), 1 Tbsp (15 ml) ketchup, splash Worcestershire sauce, pinch of cayenne, pinch of oregano, salt and pepper to taste

Horseradish: 1/4 cup (50 ml) sour cream, 1/4 cup (50 ml) mayo, 2+ Tbsp (30+ ml) horseradish (to taste), salt and pepper to taste

Steak: 1/4 cup (50 ml) sour cream, 1/4 cup (50 ml) mayo, 1 Tbsp (15 ml) Montreal Steak Spice

Buffalo: 1/2 cup (125 ml) sour cream, 1/4 cup (50 ml) ranch dressing, 1/4 cup (50 ml) hot sauce (or to taste)

Onion Blossom

Poutine

Poutine is.. well, honestly it's probably the nastiest thing ever. It's a 2am-going-home-from-the-bar kinda food. There is nothing redeeming in nutrition OR appearance. It's not haute cuisine in the slightest. It may just end up clogging your arteries on sight. Sometimes, I'm kinda embarrassed that it's sort of looked at as our national dish in Canada.

Oh, but it can be soooo good!

Done right, when you're in the right mood for it, it can take the concept of "comfort food" to whole new levels. I'm pretty sure that making it for a boyfriend has a high chance of resulting in a marriage proposal – I know my husband would marry me all over again for poutine. (He actually proposed because I made him a sandwich. No joke – it was a muffaletta.)

Poutine is a pretty simple dish from Quebec, consisting of fries, cheese curds, and "gravy". Sorry, I have to put that in quotes, as I'm a gravy snob. The most popular – and "correct" way of making the sauce, in Canada, is to use a packet mix. I'm vehemently opposed to pretty much any sauce that comes from a powder (Aside from Swiss Chalet sauce, which I would probably *drink* if presented the opportunity), so here is how I make it, from scratch. Very much worth it!

A few notes, as I tend to bastardize things up quite a bit to suit my tastes:

- Traditionally, the sauce is a chicken based velouté sauce. I've *always* preferred a beef based sauce, as I find it has more flavour.

- The sauce is something that would make any foodie turn up their nose. Seriously, this is the closest thing to authentic that you're going to get. I don't want anyone to think that this is the sort of gravy that I turn out for anything other than Poutine. LOL

- Bacon and green onions are totally optional, it's just the way I like it. I just figure A.) If you're going this far anyway, might as well add bacon!, and B.) I love the extra flavour from the green onions. Feel free to omit either/both per your tastes.

- Cheese curds should be as fresh as humanly possible – a couple days old at max, if at all possible. Freshness and bringing them to room temperature ensures a nice squeak!

- Traditionally, poutine is made with a very light (blond) roux. Well, I prefer a darker roux (more flavour!), which this recipe is based on. The lighter the roux, the more thickening power, so if you want to go lighter, you'll need a bit more broth than this recipe calls for.

- As with most of my "recipes" at home, I usually don't measure anything. I did measure for the sauce this time around, to give you a base idea of what works. This makes enough sauce for 3-4 servings, feel free to double the recipe as needed. Other ingredients, just eyeball it all. You know how many fries you'd like in a serving!

Poutine

Russet Potatoes, scrubbed clean
Cheese curds – about a handful per serving.
Bacon - as much as you'd like

Butter	1/4 cup	50 ml
Brown Rice Flour	1/4 cup	50 ml
Corn starch	1 Tbsp	15 ml
Beef broth	2 cups	500 ml
Chicken broth	1 cup	250 ml
Garlic cloves, pressed	2	2
Salt and pepper		
Oil for deep frying		
Green onions, thinly sliced		

Cut potatoes into french fries, place into a bowl of cold water for about an hour. Remove cheese curds from fridge, allow to come to room temperature as you work on everything else.

Chop bacon into small pieces, fry until crisp. Set aside

In a saucepan, melt the butter over medium-low heat. Add rice flour, corn starch, and pepper, stir well until fully incorporated. Continue to cook, stirring constantly, until flour mixture becomes the colour of peanut butter. This is called a roux, and cooking it to this level will impart a nice, somewhat nutty flavour to the sauce.

Once roux has obtained the right colour, slowly add broth. It will steam like CRAZY, so be careful. Stir as you go, until sauce is smooth. Taste, season with salt and pepper as needed. Allow to simmer on medium heat for a few minutes, until slightly thickened. This is NOT supposed to be a thick gravy! Once the sauce is a good consistency, remove from heat and set aside.

Heat oil to 325 F (165 C)

Remove fries from water, blot dry. In small batches, cook fries for 10 minutes. This will NOT brown them, merely cook them. As each batch comes out, put aside.

Once all fries are par-cooked / blanched, turn the heat up to 375 f (190 C), and allow oil to reach temperature. In small batches, re-fry the potatoes until browned and crispy, about 3-5 minutes per batch.

Yes, it seems a little involved – but this is how to get fries that are cooked all the way through, and crispy on the outside!

To assemble the Poutine:

Mound hot fries on serving plate. Add a handful of cheese curds, stir slightly. Smother with sauce, top with bacon & green onions. Serve immediately.. then maybe call your cardiologist :)

Tortillas

In getting ready to write this book, one of the most popular requests was for a great tasting tortilla that didn't rip. Seems like this recipe is a bit of a "holy grail" for a lot of people!

I've got to say... I was eating a lot of great gluten-free food while developing this book, so I was pretty spoiled by the time I got to making tortillas. Nothing could have prepared me for how great it was to have a proper burrito for supper that night. I think I'd gotten to the point of taking things for granted, you know? I guess I'd managed to forget just how great a GOOD burrito could be, it had been so long!

Makes 6-8 8" tortillas

Sorghum flour	1/2 cup	125 ml
Light buckwheat flour	1/2 cup	125 ml
White rice flour	1/2 cup	125 ml
Sweet rice flour	1/4 cup	50 ml
Tapioca starch	1/4 cup	50 ml
Granulated sugar	1 tsp	5 ml
Xanthan gum	2 tsp	10 ml
Salt	3/4 tsp	3 ml
Baking powder	1/2 tsp	2 ml
Shortening or lard	1/4 cup	50 ml
Cold water	1 cup	250 ml
Corn starch for rolling		

In a large bowl, whisk together dry ingredients until very well incorporated.

Add shortening/lard to the bowl. Use a potato masher or pastry knife to cut the shortening down to small, irregular pieces - mix should look sort of like gravel.

Add water, stir until well mixed. Knead a few times, just to bring it together - don't over work it! Wrap in dough in plastic film, allow to rest on your counter for 30 minutes.

Generously sprinkle clean work surface with corn starch. Separate dough into 4 equal sized chunks.

One chunk at a time, roll dough out as thin as possible, srinkling more corn starch as necessary. Cut an 8" round - I like to use a plate or cake pan as a guide - set aside. Collect cuttings from each round, knead together and roll to cut more rounds from. Repeat until all the dough is cut into circles.

Cook for 2-3 minutes each side in a smoking hot skillet. Cover freshly cooked torillas with a towel, repeating until all tortillas are cooked.

Serve right away, or store in an airtight container for a day or two. Reheat to soften, before use.

Tortillas

85

Pepper Cheese Dip

Most cheese dips begin as a rough Béchamel sauce - with flour as the thickener. Whether you're looking for a crock pot dip to take to a party, or a fondue for two, this is a great basic recipe to play with... and no one will miss the flour.

Gluten-free beer*	12 oz	375 ml
Red bell pepper, finely chopped	1	1
Jalapeno peppers, finely chopped	2	2
Garlic cloves, pressed	2	2
Marble Jack cheese, shredded	1 lb/ 4 cups	500 g / 1000 ml
Corn starch 2 tbsp		

In a medium saucepan, combine beer, peppers, and garlic. Bring to a boil, turn heat down, and simmer for 5 minutes. Remove from heat, allow to steep for 10 minutes.

Return pot to burner, bring back up to a simmer.

As pepper beer mixture is heating up, toss shredded cheese with cornstarch until evenly coated. Add a large handful of cheese to hot beer mixtire, stir until melted. Continue adding rest of cheese – a handful at a time – stirring until it's melted each time. Stop when dip reaches desired thickness.

Allow dip to heat for another minute or so, after the final batch of cheese. Serve warm, with corn chips.

* Not a fan of beer, or looking for an alcohol-free alternative? Use milk or chicken broth.

Variations:

- Change the cheese!

- Add more peppers, or get rid of the bell peppers in favour of more jalapenos (I like a jalapeno-cheddar dip, myself!)

- Toss in a handful of chopped cilantro just before serving

- Season with a little cumin powder, to taste

- Reduce beer to 1/2 cup (125 ml), add 1 cup (250 ml) of your favourite salsa or chili!

- Want an elegant fondue? Skip the peppers, substitute beer with white wine and/or chicken broth (you can mix the two). Use Gruyere cheese, add a pinch of nutmeg. Serve with apple, pears, celery, and gluten-free bread cubes

Pepper Cheese Dip

Tempura
88

Tempura

Tempura is a lot of fun, and makes for an easily customizable appetizer (or meal!) option. There is a wide variety of foods that you can batter and fry with this method. The beauty of going gluten free with the tempura batter is that you don't have the worry of over developing the gluten. With traditional tempura, overdeveloping the gluten (by stirring too much) causes the batter to be more doughy, rather than light and airy.

To start, prepare a selection of vegetables and/or seafood.

Vegetables:
Broccoli: Separated into florets
Butternut Squash: Thin slices or fingers
Carrot, Eggplant, Sweet Potato: Thinly sliced (1/8")
Green beans: As-is
Mushrooms: Washed, whole or halved.
Onions: Sliced, separated into individual rings
Zucchini - cut into spears

Seafood:
Crab: Whole soft shell crabs, or leg meat spears
Fish: Cut into nuggets
Sea scallops: Split in half (2 thinner circles)
Shrimp/Prawn: Peeled and deveined (usually with tail left on). For straight lengths of shrimp tempera, make a series of small cuts along the inside curve of the shrimp. Be careful not to cut all the way through!

Once your vegetables and seafood are prepared, heat vegetable oil to 375F (190 C). You can use a deep fryer, or a heavy pan. If not using a deep fryer, use a deep, heavy pot, filled to at least 3" deep. As oil is heating, prepare your batter:

White rice flour	2 cups	500 ml
Corn starch	1 cup	250 ml
Salt	1 tsp	5 ml
Baking soda	1/2 tsp	2 ml
Large egg	1	1
COLD seltzer water or club soda	2 cups	500 ml

Whisk together dry ingredients. Add egg, whisk until well combined. Add a small amount of seltzer water , stirring to combine. Continue adding seltzer water, stirring gently until just combined - mixture can be a bit lumpy. For best results, set bowl of batter in another, larger bowl that is filled with ice. The colder the batter, the better the tempura!

Gently dip vegetable and seafood pieces in the batter one at a time, slowly removing from the batter and allowing excess to drip off. Carefully transfer to heated oil. Fry a few at a time - turning every few minutes - until very lightly golden, about 2-3 minutes. Transfer fried pieces to platter lined with paper towels. Salt lightly - if you'd like - and serve hot!

Stuffing

This recipe is a bit different from the others in the book, in that it's the only one to start with a pre-made gluten-free bread product. Here's the thing: gluten free stuffing mixes are crap, making a fresh loaf of gf bread just to make stuffing is too much work.

Pre-made GF bread may be only *barely* fit for eating on its own, but with a slightly different technique than using regular bread to make stuffing, you can make something almost indistinguishable from "the real thing". Like most other gluten free recipes, this comes down to moisture, absorption, and technique.

Gluten free bread of choice	1 loaf	1 loaf
Butter	1/2 cup	125 ml
Large onions	2	2
Garlic cloves, pressed or minced	2	2
Celery stalks	3	3
Baby bella mushroom slices	8 oz	250 g
Chicken broth	1-2 cups	250-500 ml
Fresh sage, chopped	~1 oz	~ 30 g
Pepper, to taste		
2 large eggs, beaten		

Slice bread, chop or rip into small, bite-sized pieces.

In a large pot, melt butter. Add onions, garlic, mushrooms and celery, cook until veggies start to soften. Add a bit of chicken stock, Cook till everything is soft.

Rip the bread up into small chunks, add chopped sage. Toss till the sage is spread out through the bread, Add as much pepper as you figure you'd want, but don't go overboard!

Add bread mix to pot, toss to coat. Whisk eggs into remaining soup stock, pour over the bread, continue cooking until it's all absorbed.

For use in poultry: Stuff into the bird and roast as usual.

To use outside of poultry: Transfer stuffing to a large baking pan, cover with tin foil. Bake at 350 F (180 C) for about 30 minutes. Remove foil and bake another 15 minutes or so, until golden brown.

Variations:

- Swap the sage out in favour of a few handfuls of dried savoury

- Add roasted chest nuts, pine nuts, or walnuts

- Add whatever fresh herbs you like!

Stuffing

Main Dishes

Fried Chicken

Fried chicken! What all can I even say about this? To be completely honest, while the chicken turned out amazing - full of flavour, juicy, and definitely indistinguishable from the "Real" thing.. I was super distracted by the accidental coleslaw that I whipped up just to make the plate look prettier!

About 10 chicken pieces to fry - thighs, drumsticks, breasts, etc
Salt

Large eggs	4	4
Milk	1/3 cup	75 ml
Cornstarch	1 cup	250 ml
Millet flour	1/2 cup	125 ml
Sorghum flour	1/2 cup	125 ml
White rice flour	1/4 cup	50 ml
Baking powder	1 tsp	5 ml
Pepper	1 tsp	5 ml
Salt	1/2 tsp	2 ml
Dried sage	1/2 tsp	2 ml
Paprika	1/4 tsp	1 ml
Onion powder	1/4 tsp	1 ml
Garlic powder	1/4 tsp	1 ml

Arrange chicken on a baking sheet, season well with salt and place in the fridge - uncovered - for one hour.

In one large bowl, whisk together eggs and milk, set aside. In a separate large bowl, whisk together dry ingredients until well combined. Lightly dredge all rested chicken in flour mixture, shaking excess flour mixture back into the bowl. Measure about 1 Tbsp (15 ml) of milk/egg mixture into the dry ingredients. Use your fingers to work the moisture in to the dry mixture, creating some small lumps throughout.

One piece at a time, dip chicken into egg mixture, and then into flour mixture. Press flour mixture firmly against the chicken to adhere, arrange on a baking sheet. Once all chicken has been dipped and coated, allow to rest for 15 minutes.

Heat oil 325 F (165 C) You can use a deep fryer, or a heavy pan. If not using a deep fryer, use a deep, heavy pot, filled to at least 3" deep.

Once oil reaches temperature, fry chicken in batches until nicely browned and crispy. This should take between 10-14 minutes, depending on the size/type of chicken pieces. Allow oil to come back up to temperature between batches. Serve hot!

Marie's Colourful Coleslaw

This recipe was a total accident. I had just finished developing the fried chicken recipe, and needed something for the plate. Fried chicken is just so brown and blah when it comes to photos.

I decided that what it needed was probably coleslaw. Regular coleslaw adds a little colour, and you can have a bit more if you add, say, carrots.. but I wanted a LOT of colour. So, I decided to whip up a coleslaw just for the photo, with the focus being on bright colours. I had no plans to actually include a recipe for it, it was basically going to be a prop… almost like using a garnish to bring some colour.

Well, I'm really glad that I actually wrote down what I did, because it was FABULOUS. Not only was it gorgeous, it had amazing texture and a ton of flavour.. as well as a bit of kick. It was perfect! It went from being "throw something together to look pretty on the side of the plate", to being our go-to coleslaw recipe!

Napa cabbage, thinly sliced	1 small	1 small
Shredded purple cabbage	1 1/2 cup	375 ml
Carrot, peels and grated	1	1
Anaheim peppers, thinly sliced	2-3	2-3
Green onions, thinly sliced	2	2
Mayonnaise	1 cup	250 ml
Cider vinegar	1/2 cup	125 ml
Granulated sugar	2 Tbsp	30 ml
Salt	1/2 tsp	2 ml
Pepper	1/2 tsp	2 ml
Celery seed	1/2 tsp	2 ml

In a large bowl, gently toss prepared cabbages, carrot, peppers and green onions. Set aside.

In a separate bowl, whisk together remaining ingredients. Pour over vegetables, toss to coat evenly.

Cover, chill for at least 1 hour to let flavours mingle. Serve cold

Fried Chicken & Colourful Coleslaw

Singapore Mai Fun

Mei Fun? Mei Fan? Mai fan? Seems like there are a million ways to spell this, and I have NO idea which is right! I would guess "Mai Fun", but the restaurant I usually order this at, it's "Mai Fan". Ack! No matter how you spell it, this is my very favorite Asian takeout dish of all time. I'll never forget the first time I had it – I'd made the mistake of ordering it "hot", and… I've never been in so much spice-related pain in my life. My mouth was burning, and I SWEAR my tears had fire in them, also. It took hours to dissipate.

… holy crap, was it EVER good, though!

From then on – til I moved to Minnesota, anyway – whenever, wherever I ordered it, I asked for "medium" heat. (In Minnesota, "hot" means something very different than the rest of the world, and you basically have to specify "Hot-hot, not "Minnesota hot"!). SO good.

Feeling too lazy to go out one day, I decided to make my own "wing it" version. While this won't leave you in pain for hours, this version is full of flavour and sure to become a favorite for any fan of the dish.

Makes 4 servings

Boneless, skinless chicken breasts	1/2 – 1 lb	250-500 g
Lean pork	1/2 -1 lb	250-500 g
Mai fan noodles	1 package	1 package
Pan spray		
Large eggs	2	2
Hot curry powder	½ tsp	2 ml
Salt	pinch	pinch
Olive or vegetable oil, divided	2 Tbsp	30 ml
Raw shrimp, shells removed.	1/2 lb	250 g
Small onion, cut into strips	1	1
Celery ribs, thinly sliced	2-3	2-3
Fresh bean sprouts	1 cup	250 ml
Hot curry powder	1 Tbsp	15 ml
Dried hot pepper flakes	1 tsp+	5 ml+
ginger powder	1/2 tsp	2 ml
chicken stock or broth	1/2 cup	125 ml
Gluten-free soy sauce	3 Tbsp	45 ml
Rice vinegar	1 tsp	5 ml
Salt	1/2 tsp	2 ml
Green onions, thinly sliced	3	3

Cut chicken breasts into bite sized pieces, Trim pork and cut into thin strips, set aside.

Place mai fan noodles in a pot or heat safe bowl. Cover with very hot water, allow to soften for 10 minutes. Drain well, set aside.

Spray a LARGE pan (or wok) with pan spray. Whisk eggs, 1/2 tsp (2 ml) curry powder, and salt together. Pour into frying pan, cook until solid enough to flip. Flip, heat until cooked through. Transfer to a plate, cut into chunks.

Heat 1 Tbsp oil in frying pan. Cook the chicken and pork together, until almost cooked through. Add shrimp, cook just until shrimp is fully cooked (pink). Remove from heat, add to plate with egg.

Heat another 1 Tbsp oil in the frying pan. Saute onion and celery together for about 1 minute. Add bean spouts, remaining curry powder, hot pepper flakes, and ginger – toss to combine.

Add drained noodles, chicken stock, soy sauce, rice vinegar, and salt, toss to combine. Cook until almost all liquid is absorbed. Add egg, chicken, pork, and shrimp, continue cooking until everything is heated through and liquid is fully absorbed – about another minute. Remove from heat, stir in green onions, and serve hot!

Chicken Fingers

When it comes to cravings after everything "got taken away from me", one of the weirdest ones was fast food chicken nuggets. I know, it's not even really chicken - and not really food, when you think about it - but just the idea of that coherent, crispy batter over soft "chicken"? It got to me.

So, I designed this chicken finger recipe to mimic that style of coating, rather than a crumb coating. So good - especially with whole pieces of real chicken being involved! Keep in mind what I said earlier about batters not necessarily behaving the same as normal batters. This will seem really heavy, goopy, and possibly a little annoying to work with, as you dip the chicken... but I promise that the finished result is worth it!

This is a great base recipe - I like to keep my chicken finger batter relatively plain, as I like the honey dill sauce (my dip of preference!) to really sing... but you can add whatever seasonings you like - paprika, powdered Parmesan cheese, smoked serrano powder, whatever!

Garbanzo (chickpea) flour	1 1/4 cups	300 ml
Rice flour	1/4 cup	50 ml
Salt	1 tsp	5 ml
Mustard powder	1/2 tsp	2 ml
Baking powder	1/4 tsp	1 ml
Water	1 cup	250 ml
Boneless, skinless chicken breasts	3-4 Large	3-4 Large
Additional garbanzo flour	1/4 cup	50 ml

Start heating your vegetable oil to 375F (190 C) – you'll want at least 2-3" of oil in your pot or deep fryer.

In a large bowl, combine flours, salt, mustard powder and baking powder. Add water, stir well to form a thick batter. All batter to sit for 5 minutes or so, to soften the bean flour.

Slice your chicken breasts into fingers or nuggets, toss with additional garbanzo flour, then dredge in the batter. Carefully transfer a few battered chicken fingers to the preheated oil. Fry for a few minutes on each side, until golden brown and cooked through. Use a slotted metal spoon to transfer fried chicken to paper towels. Serve hot, with dipping sauce(s) of your choice.

Honey Dill Dipping Sauce

Honey dill sauce is one of those things that I grew up with, and really thought of it as being ubiquitous until I left my hometown - Winnipeg. It was only then, that I realized it's very much a regional thing.

So, let me introduce you to honey dill sauce. This is VERY much a Winnipeg thing, and "popular" doesn't even begin to describe it. If you order chicken fingers anywhere in Winnipeg, there IS honey dill sauce. Actually, not even "there IS", more like "There MUST BE". Major chain restaurants, little diners, festival food trucks, school cafeterias… it's just what you do. Kids love it, adults love it… and after putting together this post, I'm gonna NEED to make some for supper tonight!

I once saw a list of "You know you're from Winnipeg WHEN", and one of the statements was "You dip everything in Honey Dill sauce". Well, while I wouldn't go so far as to say "everything", it really is a versatile condiment. The most popular use, as I mentioned, is for chicken fingers. It's also great on roasted potato chunks, steamed carrots, salmon, egg rolls, perogies, for crudite plates … and as a french fry dip!

Makes 1 cup

Mayonnaise	2/3 cup	150 ml
Honey (Liquid, not whipped)	1/3 cup	75 ml
Dried dill	1 Tbsp	15 ml

Mix together the mayonnaise and honey until smooth and well blended. Crush the dried dill in your hand (to release more flavour), add to the mayonnaise mixture, stir well. Refrigerate for at least an hour to allow flavours to blend.

Chicken Fingers with Honey Dill Dipping Sauce

Perogies

Perogies

Growing up, my grandmother used to make amazing perogies, and I've never forgotten that – most else pales in comparison! When going gluten-free, good, Winnipeg-style perogies was one of those "holy grail" kind of recipes. While the filling is gf by default, that dough would take some doing - it had to have good flavour, be easy to work with, roll out well, and be strong enough to hold up to both boiling AND pan frying.

Of all the recipes in the book, this one had the most colourful reaction to success. It started out well - the dough rolled out paper thin, and provoked a Facebook status of "LOOK AT THE BEAUTIFUL DOUGH BEHAVING ITSELF BECAUSE IT KNOWS WHO IS BOSS HERE!" Once they were assembled, boiled, and fried... all hell broke loose. I shrieked at my husband that he had to try them, there MAY have been a declaration of being "The Tony Stark of gluten-free"... a few excited expletives, a demand to play some AC/DC. yeah. COLOURFUL. They were SO perfect.

ANYWAY. One of the beautiful things about perogies is that you can customize your fillings in SO many ways. Potato and cheddar is most traditional, where I'm from... but you can add bacon, sauerkraut, dill, cottage cheese... in any combination. Have fun with it!

Makes about 3 dozen

Sour cream	1 cup	250 ml
Large eggs	2	2
Warm milk	1/4 cup	50 ml
Vegetable oil	1/4 cup	50 ml
Tapioca starch	2/3 cup	150 ml
Sweet rice flour	1/3 cup	75 ml
Potato starch	1/3 cup	75 ml
Corn starch	1/3 cup	75 ml
Sorghum flour	1 cup	250 ml
Salt	½ tsp	2 ml
Xanthan gum	2 tsp	10 ml

In a food processor or stand mixer, blitz/beat sour cream, eggs, milk, and oil together until well combined.

In a separate bowl, whisk together remaining ingredients (except potato starch) until well combined. Add to wet ingredients, blitz/beat until a sticky dough comes together. Wrap dough in plastic film, allow to rest on counter for 45 minutes. While waiting, work on the filling:

Basic Filling:

Red potatoes, peeled and quartered	1 1/2 lbs	750 g
Cheddar cheese, shredded	1/2- 3/4 lb	250 - 375 g
Optional flavourings*		

101

Boil potatoes until fork tender and ready to mash. I like to use my stand mixer to mash my potatoes, and it works doubly well for this. You can, however, always mash and mix by hand. Either way, mash potatoes until smooth, and mix in your choice of cheese and flavourings until well incorporated

*Ideas for fillings:

Traditional: Sharp Cheddar cheese.

Onion, Bacon, and Cheese: 3/4 lbs (375 g) cheddar cheese of your choice, 1/2 lb (250 g) crisp bacon (crumbled), chopped onion to taste.

Sauerkraut: Add 1/2 lb *250 g) sauerkraut to your potatoes. Cheese is optional – up to you!

Cottage Cheese, Onion, and Dill: 1/2 lb (250 g) well drained cottage cheese, finely chopped onion and dill weed to taste.

Assembly:

1. Dust clean work surface generously with potato starch. Roll out dough, aiming to get it pretty thin – 1/16 – 1/8" of an inch or so. When you're first starting out, a bit thicker is ok – you'll just have a bit more dough to bite through to get to your yummy filling!

2. Cut dough with large glass or round cookie cutter – I like to use a glass that's about 3" in diameter.

3. Place about 1 tbsp of filling in the center of each round:

4. Lightly brush the edges with water, which will act as a glue.

5. Pick 1 round up in your non-dominant hand, and use your good hand to fold the dough around the filling, sealing the edge from one side to the other. Make sure your perogies are sealed well, or they will explode when you cook them! Also, I like to flatten them out a little.

6. Have a large pot of water heated to a low boil. (Too rough of a boil will rip your perogies apart!). Drop a few perogies in at a time – our pot can take about a dozen. Cook until all rise to the surface, then for 2-3 minutes longer:

7. Removed cooked perogies from water, lightly toss with melted butter. This will prevent them from sticking together.

8. Enjoy as-is, or fry them in butter, onions.. maybe with some Kielbasa sausage… serve with some sour cream.. YUM!

Theoretically, you can freeze these (individually on a cookie sheet, then bag them together when frozen).. but unless you make several batches (or don't really like perogies!), they'll never make it to the freezer!

Grandma's Note – Grandma is very adamant that this is time consuming (wasn't really!), and that – rather than cutting the dough into rounds, taking the scraps, and re-rolling/cutting more – I should DEFINITELY use her technique. I didn't. Sorry, gramma!

What she says you should do is this: Roll your dough out, and cut into 3" strips. Cut those again into 3" squares, place filling in the middle, and fold/seal them to make triangles. Yes, it would be quicker than the rounds – I just don't have the big hatred for cutting rounds that she seems to!

Fish Sticks (and Custard!)

These are a great "grown up" alternative to the traditional mass-produced frozen fish sticks. Almonds, flax seeds, and seasonings bring a ton of flavour to the coating, and perfectly accent the fish (We used flounder). While these can be served alone, or accompanied by a traditional tartar sauce, I like to serve them with a savoury custard as a dipping sauce.

White fish fillets of choice	1 lb	500 g
Amaranth flour	1/2 cup	125 ml
Ground gluten-free crackers	1 cup	250 ml
Sliced almonds	1/2 cup	125 ml
Flax seeds (optional)	1/4 cup	50 ml
Salt	1 tsp	5 ml
Pepper	1/4 tsp	1 ml
Mustard powder	1/4 tsp	1 ml
Dried chives	1 tsp	5 ml
Garlic powder	1/2 tsp	2 ml
Zest of 1/2 lemon		
Large eggs	2	2

Preheat oven to 375F (190 C), line a baking sheet with parchment paper.

Cut fish into sticks, about 4" x 1" long. Pat dry with a paper towel, set aside. Place amaranth flour in a bowl, set aside.

Pulse crackers and nuts in food processor until ground to crumbs. Place in a large bowl, along with flax seeds (if using), salt, pepper, mustard powder, chives, and lemon zest. Stir to combine.

Whisk together the eggs in a separate bowl.

Dip the fish into the amaranth flour, gently shaking off any excess flour. Dip next in the egg, and then the nut mixture, place on baking sheet. Repeat with all remaining fish fingers.

Bake for 15-20 minutes, or until golden brown, crispy, and cooked through. Serve with savoury custard as a dip!

Savoury Custard

Originally, I'd made this as sort of a "joke" dish to serve at a Doctor Who party. I knew that I could come up with a custard that would be far more edible than the vanilla pudding it was fashioned to resemble.. but I had NO idea that I'd like it so much as to see it as a default accompaniment for fish sticks!

Butter	2 Tbsp	30 ml
Dijon mustard	1 Tbsp+	15 ml+
Lemon juice	1 tsp	5 ml
Cayenne pepper	pinch	pinch
Garlic clove, pressed	1	1
Zest of one lemon		
Dry white wine	1/4 cup	50 ml
Large egg yolks	5	5
Corn starch	1 Tbsp	15 ml
Milk	1 1/4 cup	300 ml
Parmesan cheese	2/3 cup	150 ml

In a small saucepan, melt butter over medium heat. Whisk in Dijon mustard, lemon juice and cayenne until smooth. Add garlic, lemon zest and white wine, once again whisking until smooth. Gently bring mixture up to a simmer.

While mustard wine mixture is heating up, whisk egg yolks and corn starch together in a small bowl or measuring glass. Once smooth, whisk in milk - a little at a time - until smooth and well incorporated.

Once the mustard & wine has come to a simmer, add milk mixture, quickly whisking to fully blend the two. Bring up to a simmer again, whisking constantly. As it heats up, stir in the Parmesan cheese. Continue stirring, allowing the cheese to melt and the mixture to thicken.

Once custard has thickened to your liking, remove from heat and serve. If not serving immediately, chill for future use.

Fish Sticks & Custard

Beef Stroganoff

Shortly after going gluten-free, I was craving beef stroganoff... and was a bit horrified when my husband told me that he'd never had it made from scratch. Yep, when you say "Stroganoff" to my husband, he would think "Hamburger Helper". Eek!

Stroganoff was one of those things that I cooked fairly often when I was a bit younger and living alone. It's one of those dishes that I'd just throw together, without a lot of thought as to measurements. THIS time, I made sure to measure as I went, so I could share the recipe with all of you!

Makes 4 servings

Beef sirloin	1 1/2 lbs	750 g
Olive oil	2 Tbsp	30 ml
Medium onion, thinly sliced	1	1
Baby bella mushrooms, sliced	1 lb	500 g
Beef broth	2 cups	500 ml
Garlic cloves, pressed	3	3
Dijon mustard	1 tsp	5 ml
Corn starch	1/4 cup	50 ml
White wine	1/2 cup	125 ml
Sour cream	1/2 cup	125 ml
Dried parsley	1 Tbsp	15 ml

Freeze sirloin for about 10 minutes, just long enough to make it easy to slice. Cut chilled beef into very thin slices.

Heat olive oil in a large pan, add beef and cook until well browned. Add onions and mushrooms to the pan, cook for about 3 minutes. Add broth, garlic, and Dijon mustard to the pan, stirring well to distribute.

Whisk together corn starch and white wine until smooth. Add corn starch mixture to the pan, along with sour cream and parsley, simmer till thickened. Serve over rice or gluten free noodles of choice.

Beef Stroganoff

Savoury Marbled Basil Cheesecake

Who says cheesecake is only for dessert? This savoury version is best served at least slightly warm… I like it best chilled first, and reheated to HOT in the microwave. Yum!

Crust:

Finely chopped almonds	1 1/4 cups	300 ml
Grated Parmesan cheese	1/2 cup	125 ml
Butter, melted	1/3 cup	75 ml
Pepper	pinch	pinch

Combine all ingredients until completely incorporated and moistened. Evenly distribute across the bottom of a 9" spring form pan. Press ingredients firmly, extending crust partway up the sides of the pan. Chill for at least 1 hour.

Cheesecake:

Small onion, diced	1/2	1/2
Garlic cloves, pressed	2	2
Cream cheese, softened	2 lbs	1 kg
Shredded provolone cheese	1 cup	250 ml
Sour cream	1/2 cup	125 ml
Large eggs	6	6
Heavy cream	1 cup	250 ml
Salt	1 tsp	5 ml
pepper	1/2 tsp	2 ml
fresh basil leaves	2-3 cups	500-750 ml

Preheat oven to 425 F (220 C)

Finely chop onion and garlic in a food processor. Add cream cheese, provolone, and sour cream, process until very smooth. Add eggs, blitz for a few seconds to combine. Carefully stream in heavy cream, process just until well combined and smooth. Stir in salt and pepper, Pour half of the cheese batter into a mixing bowl. Add basil leaves to remaining batter in food processor, blitz until leaves are finely chopped and well incorporated into the batter.

Gently spoon batter into prepared crust, alternating scoops of plain and basil batters. Run a clean butter knife through the batter -being careful to not disturb the crust underneath – to marble the batters.

Bake for 15 minutes. After 15 minutes, turn the oven down to 325 F (165 C) and bake for 50 minutes. Once baking time is complete, turn off the oven and allow cheesecake cake to cool – WITHOUT opening the door! – for 2 hours.

Note: While this cheesecake is fantastic as it is, it also works well when topped with any number of complementary items. Try roasted red pepper, pesto, or crumbled bacon!

Savoury Marbled Basil Cheesecake

Hearty Beef Stew

The key to a great beef stew is to not only load it with a good variety of vegetables to complement the meat, but to have a great tasting gravy. Making a proper roux - rather than just using a "raw" flour - is the secret to a great gravy. Get it as dark as possible (without burning it!) for maximum flavour!

Stewing beef, cut into chunks	4 lbs	2 kg
Vegetable oil	2 Tbsp	30 ml
Onions, chopped	3	3
Beef broth	12 cups	3 L
1 bottle dry red wine	3 cups	750 ml
Celery ribs	4-6	4-6
Dried savoury	1 Tbsp+	15 ml+
Pepper	1 Tbsp +	15 ml+
Salt, to taste		
Rutabaga, peeled and chopped	1	1
Parsnips, peeled and chopped	5	5
Carrots, peeled and sliced	6	6
Mushrooms, cut in large chunks	1 1/2 lbs	750 g
Red potatoes, cut into large chunks	3-4 lbs	1500 g - 2 kg
Fresh Brussels sprouts, halved	2-3 lbs	1 - 1 1/2 kg
Vegetable oil	2 Tbsp	30 ml
Butter	1/2 cup	125 ml
Brown rice flour	3/4 cup	175 ml
Fresh parsley, chopped	1 bunch	1 bunch

In a very large, heavy pot, brown meat in oil. Add onions, continue to cook until translucent.

Add beef broth, red wine, celery, 1 Tbsp (15 ml) each of dried savoury and black pepper, and 2 tsp (10 ml) salt. Bring up to almost a boil, reduce heat and simmer – covered – for two hours.

Remove celery from the stew, discard. Add rutabaga, parsnips, carrots, and mushrooms, continue simmering for another hour.

Add potatoes and Brussels sprouts. Cover and simmer for another hour or so. While the stew simmers, prepare your roux:

In a large heavy pot, combine vegetable oil and butter. Heat over medium until the butter melts, stir in the flour.

Without leaving your stove (Seriously!), stir the mixture constantly over medium heat until it gets quite dark – I like to get it to a reddish brown colour. It'll take time, but it's worth it – this great flavour to the stew … just don't burn it!

Stir a ladle worth of stew stock into the roux – it'll boil up and steam, don't worry. Whisk it till smooth, then add another ladle worth of stew liquid. Continue until you have a decent amount of smooth gravy. Add the gravy into the stew, stirring well to fully distribute. Stir in fresh parsley, season with salt, pepper, and additional savoury to taste.

Hearty Beef Stew

Creamy Chicken Wild Rice Soup with Dumplings

This is the ideal comfort food for a cold winter day. Rich and thick, full of good vegetables.... and dumplings! Note: the dumpling recipe will work in any stew or soup you'd like to use it in - just make sure not to lift the cover before the steaming time is up!

Olive oil	2 Tbsp	30 ml
Large onion, chopped	1	1
Chicken breast, chopped	3- 4 lbs	1500-2000 g
Garlic cloves, pressed	3	3
Carrots, sliced	3	3
Celery ribs, sliced	5	5
Uncooked wild rice	1 1/2 cups	375 ml
Chicken broth	10 cups	2 1/2 L
Red potatoes, chopped	2 lbs	1000 g
Butter	1/2 cup	125 ml
Brown rice flour	1/2 cup	125 ml
White wine	1 cup	250 ml
Heavy cream	3 cups	750 ml
Dried savoury	1 Tbsp	15 ml
Salt and pepper		

In a large, heavy pot, cook onions in olive oil until just starting to turn translucent. Add chicken breast, cook until outside browns slightly. Add garlic, carrots, and celery, cook for one minute. Add wild rice, broth, and potatoes, bring to a boil. Set a timer for 35 minutes.

While soup is boiling, make your roux:

Melt butter in a medium sized pot. Stir in flour until smooth. Cook over medium or medium-high heat, stirring constantly, until it starts to turn slightly golden. Add wine, whisk until smooth. Add cream, continue whisking until smooth. Turn heat down to lowest setting, keep warm, while making the dumplings:

1 cup Light buckwheat flour
3/4 cup Millet flour
1/4 cup Potato flour
1 Tbsp Parsley or savoury flakes
2 tsp Tapioca starch
3 tsp Baking Powder
1 tsp Salt
1/3 cup Shortening or butter
1 1/4 cup Milk or buttermilk

In a medium sized bowl, mix together flours, parsley or savoury flakes, tapioca starch, baking powder,and salt. Measure shortening/butter into the same bowl, and cut into the dry ingredients using a pastry cutter or fork(s). The idea is to work it in until it's evenly distributed throughout, in very small pieces.

Add milk/buttermilk, stir just until dough comes together. Don't over stir or beat it. If dough is too crumbly, add a small amount of extra milk. If the dough is sticky, add a small amount of flour.

When the timer goes off, add the roux mixture to the main soup pot, stirring to combine well. Add savoury, season with salt and pepper to taste. Drop rounded tablespoons worth of dough into boiling soup. Cover and simmer for 15 minutes WITHOUT LIFTING THE LID. Serve hot.

Creamy Chicken Wild Rice Soup with Dumplings

Jamaican Beef Patties

Jamaican Beef Patties

When I was in my early teens, I developed a wicked fondness for Jamaican Beef patties. They were my standard "forgot to eat lunch, stop by a gas station" go-to food, they were the perfect accompaniment for the traditional daily Slurpee (Winnipeggers know what I mean!), and they were just… my perfect comfort food.

I was pretty disappointed when I realized that beef patties were NOWHERE to be found in Minnesota.

At some point, I decided to try making my own beef patties. I looked online to see if there were any existing recipes for what *I* knew as beef patties, and ended up pretty disappointed. Overall, I could tell that none of the recipes I found would result in the right texture – kind of a creamy, pasty meat filling, NOT just regular ground beef texture – or the right spice profile.

So, of course, I created a recipe from scratch. Well, it's more of a frankenrecipe – I bastardized my uncle's pie crust recipe, converting it to a gluten-free savoury recipe with the light taste / brilliant yellow hue that I expect from a Jamaican beef patty crust. Then, for the filling, I used the basic ideas from making Cretons – a French Canadian meat spread. Oooh boy was it ever good. In particular, the filling was so ridiculously accurate, I'm amazed that any of it actually made it as far as being married with the crusts. I could have just eaten it all with a spoon.

This recipe is a bit of work, but so very worth it. Enjoy!

Makes 6 patties

Water	1/2 cup	125 ml
Large egg	1	1
Vinegar	2 tsp	10 ml
Amaranth flour	1/2 cup	125 ml
Gluten-free oat flour	1/4 cup	50 ml
Sorghum flour	1/2 cup	125 ml
Millet flour	1/2 cup	125 ml
Corn starch	1/2 cup	125 ml
Potato starch, plus extra for rolling	1/3 cup	75 ml
Tapioca starch	2 tbsp	30 ml
Curry powder	2 tsp	10 ml
Xanthan gum	2 tsp	10 ml
Turmeric	1 tsp	5 ml
Baking powder	pinch	pinch
Salt	pinch	pinch
Lard*	1/2 lb	250 g

Whisk water, egg, and vinegar together, set aside. In a larger bowl, mix together flours, starches, curry, xanthan gum, turmeric, baking powder, and salt until well combined.

Add wet ingredients to the bowl of dry ingredients, mixing with a fork until just combined. Add lard, cut in with a pastry cutter or fork gently, until it resembles gravel. Don't over handle it. In my uncle Tom's words, "Mix it with kindness"!

Gather dough into a loose ball, divide into 6 equal balls. Wrap each with plastic wrap, and let rest for 30 minutes before using.

* Shortening can be substituted if lard cannot be obtained, but is definitely not *preferable* to lard.

Filling

Large onion, finely chopped	1	1
Habanero pepper, finely chopped	1	1
Coarse ground black pepper	1 tsp	5 ml
Curry powder	1 tsp	5 ml
Salt	1 tsp	5 ml
Dried thyme	1 tsp	5 ml
Allspice	1/4 tsp	1 ml
Cloves	1/4 tsp	1 ml
Lean ground beef	1 lb	500 g
Milk	1/2 cup	125 ml
Beef broth/stock	1/2 cup	125 ml
Large egg, beaten	1	1
Water	2 Tbsp	30 ml

In a large frying pan, saute the onion and habanero pepper together until onion is translucent and soft. Add the spices, stir until well distributed.

Add in the ground beef, milk. Cook over medium heat, stirring / mashing until mixture looks relatively uniform. Add beef broth, continue to cook – stirring often – until most of the liquid has cooked off, leaving a somewhat wet paste. Cool to room temperature.

Preheat oven to 400 F (200 C), line baking sheets with parchment paper

Lightly dust your work surface with extra potato starch. Roll each of the dough balls to about 6-7" diameter.

Center about 1/2 cup of filling on each crust, moisten edges of each crust with a little water. Fold each crust in half, pushing out some of the air as you go. Press edges closed, then "crimp" by pressing down gently with a fork. Place finished pastries on prepared baking sheets.

Whisk together egg and water, lightly brush over the top of each pie.

Bake for 30-45 minutes, or until golden. Serve hot.

Tourtière

Proper Tourtière ("Tortière", for some) a wonderful thing. Tourtière is a French Canadian meat pie, and it's soooo good when made properly. There are probably as many ways to make it, as there are people in Quebec. Some people use mashed potatoes, some use cubed potatoes... some will skip the carrots, others may skip the celery. This is my way.

Ground pork	1 lb	500 g
Lean ground beef	1 lb	500 g
Small onion, finely chopped	1	1
Celery ribs, finely chopped	4	4
Carrots, grated	2	2
Fresh parsley, chopped	1/2 cup	125 ml
Potatoes, peeled, cut 1/4" cubes	2	2
Dried savoury	1-2 Tbsp	15-30 ml
Pepper	2-3 tsp	10-15 ml
Bay leaves	2	2
Salt	1 tsp	5 ml
Cloves	1/4 tsp	1 ml
Milk	2 cups	500 ml
Beef or chicken broth	1 1/2 cups	375 ml
Amaranth flour	1/2 cup	125 ml
Sorghum flour	3/4 cup	175 ml
Millet flour	1/2 cup	125 ml
Corn starch	1/2 cup	125 ml
Potato starch, plus more for rolling	1/3 cup	75 ml
Tapioca starch	2 Tbsp	30 ml
Xanthan gum	2 tsp	10 ml
Butter, softened	1/2 cup	125 ml
Cream cheese, softened	8 oz	250 g
Large egg	1	1
Large egg	1	1
Cold water	1 Tbsp	15 ml

Combine meats, vegetables, and seasonings together in a large pan or pot, stirring until everything is relatively uniform. Add the milk and the broth, stirring once again.

Bring mixture to a boil, then turn the heat down to medium and simmer – stirring often – until the liquid has cooked off, and the meat has broken down almost to a paste. This should take about an hour, give or take. Once it's ready, remove from heat and cool to room temperature.

Combine flours, starches, and xanthan gum, whisking well to combine. Set aside.

Beat butter and cream cheese until well mixed and soft. Slowly add dry ingredients, mixing until a dough comes together. Generously dust work surface with additional potato starch, turn dough out and knead until smooth. Form a disk, wrap tightly in plastic wrap, and refrigerate for about 30 minutes.

Preheat oven to 425 F (220 C)

Divide dough into 2 parts – one slightly bigger than the other. Roll the bigger section out, use it to line a deep-dish pie pan – carefully working it into the corners. Fill pie pan with meat filling, spreading it into the corners and mounding it in the center.

Roll out the second part of dough, cover the pie filling. Crimp the edges as desired, poke a couple of slits in it. If desired, roll any extra dough very thin, cut into shapes, and apply to the crust for decoration. Whisk together egg and water, brush over the entire top.

Whisk the remaining egg together with water, use a pastry brush to coat the entire crust with a thin wash of this glaze.

Bake at 20 minutes, turn heat down to 375F (190 C) and continue to bake for another 15 minutes, until crust is golden brown. Serve warm or cold.

Tourtière

Fresh Pasta

Homemade pasta may sound fancy and exotic at first, but it's actually quite easy – and can be fun, too! Regular pasta only needs two ingredients - flour and eggs. Super basic.

For gluten-free pasta, it took some experimenting to get a good dough going: one that was easy to work with, rolled out thinly, held up to boiling, and tasted great. It came down to almost the same level of ease.. "flour mixture and eggs", rather than "flour and eggs".. but hey, close enough!

Makes about 1.5 lbs of fresh pasta (before cooking)

Sorghum flour	1 cup	250 ml
Tapioca starch	2/3 cup	150 ml
Corn starch	2/3 cup	150 ml
Sweet rice flour	1/3 cup	75 ml
Xanthan gum	2 tsp	10 ml
Large eggs	7	7

Whisk all dry ingredients together until well combined. From this point, there are three main ways to make pasta with this recipe:

1. By hand. Stir your eggs into the flour mixture, use your hands to knead it into a dough.

2. By stand mixture: Dump everything in the bowl of your stand mixture, attach a dough hook, and let it do its thing.

3. In a food processor. Put all the ingredients into a food processor, let it rip.

Cover dough with plastic wrap, allow to rest for about 1 hour. Once the hour is up, bring a large pot of water to a boil - salt it well.

Dump rested dough out onto a surface that's been generously dusted with cornstarch, knead for a minute or two until soft and elastic. If it feel too sticky, add a little corn starch and knead it in.

Roll dough VERY thin, cut it into long strips. Boil pasta in batches, a few minutes per batch, until pasta floats and is desired tenderness. Serve hot with whatever sauce you'd like.

Variations:

Pesto: Use 6 eggs instead of 7. Add 1/3 cup (75 ml) finely ground pesto to the dough ingredients before combining. (Chunks of nuts will rip the dough, so you want the pesto to be a fine paste!)

Roasted and pureed vegetables: Think beets, winter squash, garlic, peppers, carrots. Roast them, peel them, and puree them into a fine paste. Use 6 eggs instead of 7, add about 1/3 cup (75 ml) of the paste to the dough ingredients before combining.

Dried herbs and spices: Add whatever you'd like to the base recipe - or to any of the variations - for a more complex flavour

Leafy greens: Spinach can be boiled for a few minutes, strained VERY well, and then pureed… but think of the other possibilities! Beet greens, kale, mustard greens – when used sparingly – can produce interesting flavours as well! Use 6 eggs instead of 7, add 1/4 - 1/3 cup (50-75 ml) of puree to the dough ingredients before combining.

For Tortellini:

Cut rolled pasta into 3" squares, drop a bit of desired filling in the middle of each – about 1/2 tsp (2 ml). Use a pastry brush to brush a little whisked egg along the edges of pasta.

Fold each piece in half to form a triangle, pushing out excess air from around the filling as you go. Press to firmly seal edges.

Fold the "top" tip of the triangle down lightly. Bend ravioli edges backwards, pressing together on the opposite side from the folded down top. Press edges firmly together to seal.

Transfer tortellini to boiling water in batches, cooking for 3-5 minutes or until they float to the surface. Strain well, serve hot!

For Ravioli:

Roll pasta into long, narrow strips, about 3-4" wide and very thin. Drop a bit of filling (1/2 – 1 tsp / 2-5 ml) along the middle of the pasta sheet, leaving an inch or two between each drop. Use a pastry brush to brush a little whisked egg around each drop of filling.

Carefully place a second sheet of thinly rolled dough on top of the first, sandwiching the filling between them. Lightly press down on the filling lumps, pressing down on the surrounding dough to seal. Be sure to push out as much air as you can, as you go. Use a knife or a pastry wheel to trim the pasta into squares. Press edges of each square firmly together to seal.

Transfer ravioli to boiling water in batches, cooking for 3-5 minutes or until they float to the surface. Strain well, serve hot!

Goat Cheese Filling:

Goat cheese	4 oz	125 g
Ricotta cheese	1/2 cup	125 ml
Salt and pepper, to taste		

Combine all ingredients until everything is well incorporated. Cover with plastic wrap and chill until use.

Sausage Filling:

Small onion	1	1
Garlic cloves	3	3
Celery rib	1/2	1/2
Olive oil	1 Tbsp	15 ml
Raw sausage meat	12 oz	375 g
Asiago cheese	1/2 cup	125 ml
Large egg	1	1
Salt, pepper		

Saute onion, garlic, and celery until tender. Remove from heat, strain, allow to cool to room temperature. Transfer sauteed vegetables, sausage, cheese, and egg to a food processor, season with a bit of salt and pepper. Blitz until well combined and smooth. Cover with plastic wrap and chill until use.

"Spanakopita" Filling (particularly good with spinach pasta):

Feta cheese	4 oz	125 g
Ricotta cheese	1 cup	250 ml
Dried dill	1 tsp	5 ml
Dried parsley	1 tsp	5 ml
Pepper	1/4 tsp	1 ml
Salt	1/4 tsp	1 ml
Nutmeg	pinch	pinch

Combine all ingredients until everything is well incorporated. Cover with plastic wrap and chill until use.

Basil Cream Sauce:

Cream cheese, softened	4 oz	125 g
Pesto	2 Tbsp	30 ml
Milk	1/2 cup	125 ml
Heavy cream	1 cup	250 ml
Salt and pepper, to taste		

In a medium saucepan, whisk cream cheese with pesto and a little heavy cream until smooth. Stream heavy cream into mixture slowly, whisking constantly to form a thick sauce. Add remaining heavy cream and milk, whisking once more until smooth and uniform.

Heat sauce, stirring often, until it comes to a simmer. Simmer for a few minutes, until thickened.

My "Alfredo" Sauce:

Butter	1/2 cup	125 ml
Corn starch	1/4 cup	50 ml
Cream cheese, softened	8 oz	250 g
Garlic cloves, pressed	10	10
Dry white wine	1 cup	250 ml
Milk	2 cups	500 ml
Shredded Parmesan cheese	2 cups	500 ml
Salt and pepper		

In a medium-large saucepan, melt butter over medium-high heat. Add corn starch, whisk well. Add cream cheese and garlic, whisk until smooth. Add wine and milk, a little at a time, whisking with each addition.   Bring just to a simmer.

Add Parmesan cheese to the pot 1 handful at a time, stirring to melt/combine. Once all of the cheese is incorporated and the sauce is smooth and silky, season with salt and pepper to taste.

Sausage Ravioli

Pickled Beet Tart

The weekend that the Kickstarter went live for this book, I debuted a cool new appetizer at a party for a ton of friends. They were mini pastry tart shells filled with a goat/ricotta cheese mousse, and topped with little wedges of picked beets, fresh pears, bits of walnuts, and ribbons of fresh basil. They were based on a salad that my husband and I had been addicted to at the time, and they FLEW off the trays.

While they looked gorgeous as they were, I thought it would be a great idea to do a larger version as a dinner serving. The mini tarts looked gorgeous, but a large tart would be much better suited for a normal dinner. Because the tart shell can be baked the night before, this can actually whip up as a fairly quick meal option. The ingredients for the toppings don't need any kind of exact measurement, just eyeball it. If you really love pickled beets, use extra. If you don't like walnuts, skip them.

White rice flour	3/4 cup	175 ml
Light buckwheat flour	3/4 cup	175 ml
Millet flour	1/2 cup	125 ml
Sweet rice flour	1/4 cup	50 ml
Corn starch, plus more for rolling	1/4 cup	50 ml
Xanthan gum	2 tsp	10 ml
Cream cheese	8 oz	250 g
Cold butter	1/2 cup	125 ml
Large egg	1	1
Cold water	1/4 cup	50 ml

Measure flours, corn starch, and xanthan gum into the bowl of your food processor, blitz to combine. Add cream cheese, butter, and egg, blitz a few times until mixture resembles gravel. Stream in cold water as you run the food processor, just long enough to bring it together as a dough.

Remove dough from processor, knead lightly to bring it together as a ball. Wrap in plastic film, chill for 1 hour.

Preheat oven to 350 F (180 C).

Generously dust work surface with corn starch, Roll chilled dough out to a rough circle that's slightly bigger than 12" in diameter. Carefully transfer rolled dough to tart pan, smoothing the bottom and pressing the dough into the sides of the pan. Trim any excess dough that extends past the top of the pan, prick the flat (bottom) surface of the crust a few times with a fork.

Bake for 20-25 minutes or until golden brown. Allow to cool to room temperature before filling.

Filling:

Goat cheese	1 cup / 8 oz	250 ml/250 g
Ricotta cheese	1/2 cup	125 ml
Heavy cream	3/4 cup	175 ml
Salt and pepper		

Using a stand or hand mixer, beat goat and ricotta cheese together until light and fluffy. Add heavy cream, beating on slow until well combined. Turn spead up and whip on high until fluffy. Season with salt and pepper to taste. Chill until ready to use.

Toppings:

Ripe pears of choice	1-2	1-2
Pickled beet slices		
Toasted walnuts		
Fresh Basil, sliced into thin ribbons (chiffonade)		

To assemble, spread filling in baked and cooled tart shell. Top with pears and beet slices, garnish with walnuts and basil. Serve immediately, or chill until ready to serve.

Pickled Beet Tart

French Onion Soup Tart

Where the pickled beet tart was inspired by a cool salad, this tart is inspired by a hot soup! I wanted to do a caramelized onion tart in general, but soon decided that I'd base all the flavours around French onion soup. I liked the idea of including a custard base, as one would normally do for *dessert* tarts .. but a savoury custard, picking up more of the flavours of French Onion soup. It's a bit of work, but easy to do - with impressive results!

Shredded Gruyere cheese	1 cup	250 ml
Light buckwheat flour	3/4 cup	175 ml
White rice flour	1/2 cup	125 ml
Sweet rice flour	1/4 cup	50 ml
Tapioca starch	1 Tbsp	15 ml
Corn starch	1/4 cup	50 ml
Xanthan gum	1 tsp	5 ml
Salt	1/2 tsp	2 ml
Baking powder	1/2 tsp	2 ml
Large egg	1	1 ml
Lard	1/2 cup	125 ml
Cold water	1/4 cup	50 ml

Measure cheese, flours, starches, xanthan gum, salt, and baking powder into the bowl of your food processor, blitz to combine. Add egg and lard to the bowl, blitz a few times until mixture resembles gravel. Stream in cold water as you run the food processor, just long enough to bring it together as a dough. Remove dough from processor, knead lightly to bring it together as a ball. Wrap in plastic film, chill for 1 hour.

Preheat oven to 350 F (180 C).

Generously dust work surface with corn starch, Roll chilled dough out to a rough circle that's slightly bigger than 12" in diameter. Carefully transfer rolled dough to tart pan, smoothing the bottom and pressing the dough into the sides of the pan. Trim any excess dough that extends past the top of the pan, prick the flat (bottom) surface of the crust a few times with a fork.

Bake for 25-30 minutes or until golden brown. While tart is baking, prepare your caramelized onions:

Butter	1/2 cup	125 ml
Sweet onions, peeled and sliced	3 lbs	1500 g
Dry white wine	1/2 cup	125 ml
Salt	1/2 tsp	2 ml
Granulated sugar	2 tsp	10 ml
Beef stock	1/2 cup	125 ml
Chopped fresh thyme	1 tsp	5 ml
Salt and pepper		

In a large pot over medium-high heat, cook onions in butter until they start to soften. Add wine and salt, continue cooking - stirring often - until nicely brown. Add sugar and beef stock to pan, stir well, and continue cooking until onions are nicely caramelized. Remove from heat, stir in fresh thyme, season with salt and pepper to taste.

Custard Filling

Butter	2 Tbsp	30 ml
Garlic cloves, pressed	2	2 ml
Dry white wine	1/4 cup	50 ml
Beef broth	1/2 cup	125 ml
Large egg yolks	5	5
Corn starch	1 Tbsp	15 ml
Milk	3/4 cup	175 ml
Shredded Gruyere cheese	1 cup	250 ml
Salt and pepper		

In a small saucepan, melt butter over medium heat. Add garlic, white wine, and beef broth, once again whisking until smooth. Gently bring mixture up to a simmer.

While wine mixture is heating up, whisk egg yolks and corn starch together in a small bowl or measuring glass. once smooth, whisk in milk - a little at a time - until smooth and well incorporated.

Once the wine mix has come to a simmer, add milk mixture, quickly whisking to fully blend the two. Bring up to a simmer again, whisking constantly. As it heats up, add the Gruyere cheese, stirring to melt and combine.

Once custard has thickened to your liking, remove from heat, season with salt and pepper to taste

For serving hot: Spread hot custard in warm crust, top with hot caramelized onions, serve immediately.

For a cold tart: Allow everything to cool to room temperature before spreading custard in crust and topping with onions. Child until serving.

French Onion Soup Tart
127

Swedish Meatballs

Gone may be the days where I could enjoy Swedish meatballs at a big department start, paying almost nothing for them... but with this recipe, I'm able to tackle that particular craving accurately, and without a ton of effort. These are great - the flax meal acts as a great binder, without getting in the way of the overall flavour profile. The nutmeg and allspice - both in the meatball and the sauce - gives the meatballs the characteristic Scandinavian flavour. For accuracy, I like to blitz these meatballs in a food processor - this produces a dense, very uniform meatball. For a more normal meatball, gentle hand mix them before rolling.

Makes about 3 dozen

Meatballs:

Olive oil, divided	2 Tbsp	30 ml
Small onion, grated	1	1
Ggarlic clove, pressed	1	1
Lean ground beef	1 lb	500 g
Ground pork	1 lb	500 g
Large egg yolks	2	2
Flax meal	1/4 cup	50 ml
Salt	1 tsp	5 ml
Pepper	1/2 tsp	2 ml
Allspice	1/4 tsp	1 ml
Nutmeg	1/4 tsp	1 ml

Sauce:

Butter	1/4 cup	50 ml
White rice flour	1/3 cup	75 ml
Beef broth	3 cups	750 ml
Sour cream	3/4 cup	175 ml
Salt and pepper to taste		
Nutmeg	pinch	pinch
Allspice	pinch	pinch

In a large nonstick pan, saute onions and garlic in 1 Tbsp of the olive oil until translucent and tender. Remove from heat, transfer to large bowl, set aside to cool.

Once onion mixture is cool enough to handle, add beef, pork, eggs, flax meal and seasonings. Using your (clean!) hands, gently mix everything together until it's all well incorporated into the mix. For tender meatballs, be gentle- you want to just mix, not squeeze and compress it much! (For the more dense, firm, and uniform meatballs, blitz in the blender til combined.)

Heat remaining oil in a large pan. Once hot, brown meatballs a few at a time, turning every so often to ensure even browning. Transfer browned meatballs to a plate as you finish each batch, leaving pan drippings.

Once all meatballs are browned and removed from the pan, add butter and white rice flour to the pan, whisking well to combine. Cook over medium heat for a few minutes, just until mixture starts to turn very pale brown - almost a straw colour. Add beef broth a little at a time, whisking till smooth. Continue cooking over medium heat just until mixture reaches a simmer. Add sour cream, whisk until completely smooth and well combined. Season with salt, pepper, nutmeg, and allspice to taste.

Add meatballs back to the pan, cover and simmer for about 10 minutes, or until cooked all the way through. Serve hot.

Swedish Meatballs

Irish Stew Meatballs

I love Irish Stew. When done properly, it's such a simple dish, but with a lot of good, "clean" flavour. It's a hearty meal that really lets the individual flavours take the spotlight: Perfectly cooked carrots and parsnips, at just the right level of tenderness... fresh parsley, good meat. Yum! I decided I'd create a meatball, themed around the flavours of Irish stew. Oh, these were fabulous... and pretty much flew out of the crock pot they were served from! The carrots, parsnips, and parsley added a ton of flavour to the meatballs, the texture was great, and it all came together perfectly!

Makes about 60 meatballs

Carrot	1	1
Parsnip	1	1
Small onion	1	1
Garlic cloves, pressed	2	2
Lean ground beef	1 1/2 lb	750 g
Ground pork	1 lb	500 g
Fresh parsley	1/4 cup	50 ml
Large eggs	2	2
Finely crushed gluten free crackers	2/3 cup	150 ml
Potato starch	1/4 cup	50 ml
Pepper	1 tsp	5 ml
Salt	1/2 tsp	2 ml
Vegetable oil	1 cup	250 ml
Beef broth	2 cups	500 ml
Potato starch	2 Tbsp+	30 ml+
Fresh parsley	1/4 cup	50 ml
Salt and pepper to taste		

Grate carrot, parsnip, and onion (I love my food processor!), place in a nonstick pan. Heat over medium, stirring frequently, until vegetables start to "sweat" out their moisture. Add garlic, continue to cook until liquid disappears. Remove from heat, transfer to a mixing bowl to cool slightly.

Once vegetables are cool enough to handle, add beef, pork, parsley, eggs, cracker crumbs, potato starch, pepper, and salt. Using your (clean!) hands, gently mix everything together until it's all well incorporated into the mix. Be gentle- you want to just mix, not squeeze and compress it much! Shape meat mixture into meatballs – about 1 1/2" in diameter. You'll end up with about 60 meatballs.

Heat vegetable oil in a large pan. Once hot, brown meatballs a few at a time, turning every so often to ensure even browning. Transfer browned meatballs to a plate as you finish each batch.

In a large pot, whisk together beef broth and potato starch until smooth. Bring to a simmer over medium heat. Add parsley, salt, and pepper, continue to cook – whisking frequently – until thickened. Add meatballs, continue to simmer for 10-15 minutes. Serve hot.

Irish Stew Meatballs

Spicy Orange Chicken

One of thing things that I miss most about my pre-gluten allergy days? Chinese takeout. I KNOW. I'm sorry! Sometimes, you just need it, you know? So, early on I decided to craft a gluten free version of.. something. I had no idea what I was specifically in the mood for. Sometimes, being able to make anything gets a bit daunting – so many options. General Tso's? Kung Pao? I wanted something a bit spicy, but wasn't quite sure which way I wanted to go.

In the end, I decided to wing it and came up with a spicy orange chicken… and it was DAMN good. Really hit the spot, and my full-gluten husband even preferred it to actual, non-gf takeout. Score! It went on to become the most popular recipe on my blog for almost a year ... so it wouldn't be right to NOT include it here!

Serves 4

Vegetable Oil for deep frying		
Garbanzo flour	1 1/4 cup	300 ml
White rice flour	1/4 cup	50 ml
Baking powder	1/4 tsp	1 ml
Salt	1 tsp	5 ml
Vegetable oil	1/2 tsp	2 ml
Water	1 cup	250 ml
Juice and zest of 2 oranges		
Gluten-free soy sauce	2 Tbsp	30 ml
Freshly grated ginger	1 Tbsp	15 ml
Garlic cloves, pressed	2-3	2-3
Hot pepper flakes	1 tsp+	5 ml+
Rice vinegar	1 Tbsp	15 ml
Honey	1/2 cup	125 ml
Corn starch	2 tsp	10 ml
Large chicken breasts, cut up	3	3
Garbanzo bean flour	1/4 cup	50 ml

Start heating your oil to 375F (190 C) – you'll want at least 2-3" of oil in your pot or deep fryer.

In a large bowl, combine flours, baking powder, salt, and vegetable oil. Add water, stir well to form a thick batter. Allow batter to sit for 5 minutes or so, to soften the bean flour.

In a medium saucepan, whisk all sauce ingredients together until smooth. Heat over medium, simmer until it thickens slightly. Remove from heat, set aside while you fry the chicken.

Toss chicken chunks with additional garbanzo flour, then dredge in the batter. Carefully transfer a few battered chicken pieces to the preheated oil. Fry for a few minutes on each side, until golden brown and cooked all the way through. Use a slotted metal spoon to transfer fried chicken to paper towels. Once all chicken is fried, toss with spicy orange sauce, serve immediately.

Spicy Orange Chicken
133

Kung Pao Chicken

This is a great, fresh version of a takeout classic. Kung Pao chicken, what else is there to say?

I do have a funny story about the creation of this recipe/photo, though. I was preparing the celery, when my husband leaned over my shoulder and declared "I love that they look like little Star Trek insignias". He proposes that - where veggies can be sliced, chopped, julienned, etc - "Star Trek" should be accepted as a new cooking verb. Ie: "Star Trek your celery before adding it to the pot".

Personally, I think I married well.

Serves 4

Boneless skinless chicken breasts	2 lb	1000g
Rice wine vinegar	1/3 cup	75 ml
Sesame oil	1/3 cup	75 ml
Garlic cloves, pressed	5	5
Grated fresh ginger	2 tsp	10 ml
Zest of one orange		
Liquid honey	2 Tbsp	30 ml
Corn starch	2 Tbsp	30 ml
Water	2 Tbsp	30 ml
Red pepper flakes	1 Tbsp +	30 ml
Small can sliced water chestnuts	1	1
Cashew pieces/halves (or peanuts)	1/2 cup	125 ml
Green onions, thinly sliced	3-4	3-4
Celery ribs, "Star Trekked"	2	2

Cut chicken breasts into bite sized chunks, place in a glass bowl or other wessel to marinate. In a separate bowl, combine rice wine vinegar, sesame oil, garlic, ginger, and orange juice, whisk well to combine. Pour over chicken, cover, and marinate for 1 hour.

Transfer chicken and marinade to a large nonstick pan or wok. Over medium-high heat, cook chicken until browned and almost cooked through.

While chicken is cooking, whisk together honey, corn starch, water, and red pepper flakes. Once chicken has browned, pour this sauce into the pan, stirring to coat the chicken. Turn heat down to medium, add remaining ingredients, and simmer for a few minutes - just until chicken is fully cooked, and sauce has thickened.

Serve hot

Kung Pao Chicken

Sesame Chicken

Be forewarned: this recipe will likely wreck you for all other sesame chicken, whether you're gluten-free or not. There are NO words for how much better homemade is, than anything we've ever had from takeout restaurants. The sweetness and spice levels are perfect, the chicken was super juicy and much higher quality than most takeout places offer, and there wasn't the "I think this may have been sitting for a few hours" texture. SO good. If you're a fan of sesame chicken, you need to make this ASAP.

Makes 4-6 servings

Oil for deep frying – we used vegetable oil

Garbanzo flour	3/4 cup	175 ml
Corn starch	1/2 cup	125 ml
White rice flour	1/4 cup	50 ml
Baking powder	1/4 tsp	1 ml
Salt	1 tsp	5 ml
Sesame oil	1 tsp	5 ml
Water or chicken broth	1 cup	250 ml
Chicken broth	1 cup	250 ml
Brown sugar, packed	1/2 cup	125 ml
Rice vinegar	2 Tbsp	30 ml
Gluten-free soy sauce	2 Tbsp	30 ml
Freshly grated ginger	1 Tbsp	15 ml
Garlic cloves	2	2
Corn starch	2 Tbsp	30 ml
Sesame oil	1 Tbsp	15 ml
Crushed pepper flakes	1 tsp	5 ml
Chicken breasts, cut into chunks	4	4
Garbanzo bean flour	1/4 cup	50 ml
Sesame seeds	2 Tbsp	30 ml

Start heating your oil to 375F (190 C) – you'll want at least 2-3" of oil in your pot or deep fryer.

In a large bowl, combine flours, baking powder, salt, and vegetable oil. Add water, stir well to form a thick batter. All batter to sit for 5 minutes or so, to soften the bean flour.

In a medium saucepan, whisk all sauce ingredients together until smooth. Heat over medium, simmer until it thickens slightly. Remove from heat, set aside while you fry the chicken.

Toss chicken chunks with additional garbanzo flour, then dredge in the batter. Carefully transfer battered chicken pieces to the preheated oil, cooking in batches. Fry for a few minutes on each side, until golden brown and cooked all the way through. Use a slotted metal spoon to transfer fried chicken to paper towels. Once all chicken is fried, toss with sauce, sprinkle with sesame seeds, and serve immediately.

Sesame Chicken

137

Seafood Crepes

When I was in my young teens, a local breakfast restaurant offered seafood crepes on the menu. It wasn't anything fancy or refined - I think it actually used those fake crab sticks - but I loved it. As an adult, I decided that I should make a more elegant version as a supper option - better seafood, some white wine... oh, it's delicious.

When preparing the crepes to use in this recipe, I like to substitute dry white wine for the water in the crepes recipe.

Makes 4 servings

Crab claw meat	6 oz	170 g
Shrimp peeled and deveined	1 lb	500 g
Bay scallops, raw	1 lb	500 g
Olive oil	1 Tbsp	15 ml
Small onion, chopped	1/2	1/2
Garlic cloves, crushed	1-2	1-2
Cream cheese, softened	8 oz	250 g
Dry white wine	1/2 cup	125 ml
Heavy cream	1/2 cup	125 ml
Shredded Parmesan cheese	1 cup	250 ml
1 prepared batch basic crepes, page 33		
Thinly sliced green onion, optional	1/2 cup	125 ml

Strain any excess liquid off crab meat, if applicable. Pick through meat to remove shells, discard any found. Combine crab meat, shrimp, and scallops in a large bowl, set aside.

In a large nonstick pan, saute onion and garlic in oil, cooking over medium-high heat until onions are tender and translucent. Add cream cheese, whisk until smooth. Add wine, heavy cream, and Parmesan, stir til smooth. Add seafood, cook just until seafood is cooked through.

Fill crepes with hot seafood mixture, allowing two crepes per person. Garnish with additional shredded Parmesan cheese, or with sliced green onions. Serve hot.

Seafood Crepes

Crab Cakes

These crab cakes are everything you could want in a crab cake - flavourful, colourful, very quick and easy to make. The ingredients come together quickly, and cooking takes no time. The result is a meal that is elegant and impressive for entertaining, but still suitable as a quick and relatively healthy weeknight meal.

Makes about 4 servings

Crab meat	1 lb	500 g
Mayonnaise	1/4- 1/2 cup	50-125 ml
Large eggs, beaten	2	2
Dijon mustard	1 Tbsp	15 ml
Worcestershire sauce	1 tsp	5 ml
Garlic clove, pressed	1	1
Salt	1/2 tsp	2 ml
White rice flour	1/3 cup	75 ml
Green onions, finely chopped	3	3
Fresno chili, finely chopped	1	1
Vegetable oil		
Lemon, sliced into wedges	1	1

Strain any visible liquid off crab meat, if applicable. Pick through meat to remove shells, discard any found. Set crab meat aside.

In a large bowl, whisk together mayonnaise, eggs, and mustard until smooth. Add Worcestershire sauce, garlic, salt, and rice flour, once again whisking until smooth and well incorporated. Add green onions, chili, and crab meat, gently mix until well combined. Cover and chill for 1 hour.

In a large fry pan, heat 1-2 Tbsp oil over medium heat. As oil is heating, shape crab mixture into patties.

Use a metal spatula to gently transfer crab cakes to oil, being careful not to burn yourself - oil may spatter. Pan fry crab cakes until browned - about 4 minutes on each side.

Serve warm, with lemon wedges

Crab Cakes

Fish and Chips

Having spent some time on the east coast, I KNOW good fish and chips. Crispy, golden batter, encasing tender, juicy fish. Personally, I'm a fan of Atlantic Cod, but Pacific cod works well too.

Douse it in proper vinegar... oh yeah. This recipe will NOT disappoint even those who are fish N Chips purists.

Now, vinegar can be a bit of a sticking point for some. Much like with whiskey, most experts/associations agree that all vinegar is gluten free - even malt vinegar, which is distilled from a wheat preparation. However, some people find themselves reacting to malt vinegar - so exercise caution.

Garbanzo (chickpea) flour	1 1/2 cups	375 ml
Rice flour	1/2 cup	125 ml
Baking powder	1 Tbsp	15 ml
Salt	1 tsp	5 ml
Pepper	1/2 tsp	2 ml
Onion powder	1/4 tsp	1 ml
Garlic powder	1/4 tsp	1 ml
Large egg, beaten	1	1
Cold gluten-free beer	1 1/2 cups	375 ml
Boneless cod fillets or loins	1-2 lbs	500-1000 g
Salt and pepper		
Garbanzo flour, for dredging	1 cup	250 ml
Fries, recipe on page 81		

Start heating your oil to 350F (180 C) – you'll want at least 2-3" of oil in your pot or deep fryer.

In a large bowl, combine flours, baking powder, salt, pepper, and onion/garlic powders. Add egg and beer, stir well to form a thick batter. All batter to sit for 5 minutes or so, to soften the bean flour.

Season fish fillets with salt and pepper. Gently dredge fish in garbanzo flour, shaking excess flour back into the bowl. One piece at a time, dip into batter, allowing excess batter to drip back into bowl for a few seconds, before carefully transferring to heated oil.

Fry for a few minutes on each side, until golden brown and cooked through. Use a slotted metal spoon to transfer fried fish to paper towels. Allow oil to come back up to temperature between batches.

Serve hot, with fries.

Fish and Chips

143

Cream of Mushroom Soup

Mushroom soup is one of those great comfort foods from our childhoods... but that can be done far better when made from scratch. Gluten free or not, homemade mushroom soup is easy to make and absolutely delicious - definitely a few steps up from the canned variety.

Makes 6-8 servings

Olive oil	1 Tbsp	15 ml
Small onion, finely chopped	1	1
Garlic cloves, pressed	2	2
Button mushrooms, sliced	1 lb	500 g
Baby bella mushrooms, sliced	1/2 lb	250 g
Dry white wine	1 cup	250 ml
Chicken broth	6 cups	1 1/2 L
Butter	1/4 cup	50 ml
White rice flour	1/4 cup	50 ml
Heavy cream	2 cups	500 ml
Dried thyme	1/4 tsp	1 ml
Salt and pepper, to taste		

In a large pot, saute onion in olive oil til soft. Add garlic and mushrooms, saute for one minute. Add white wine and chicken broth, simmer for 5-10 minutes or until mushrooms are quite soft. Remove about half the mushrooms, set aside. Puree remaining mushrooms in broth until smooth. Return to heat, add reserved mushrooms back into the pot.

In a separate small saucepan, melt butter. Add white rice flour, whisk well until well combined. Add cream, whisking well until smooth. Bring just to a simmer before adding mixture to pot of mushrooms. Season with thyme, salt, and pepper to taste. Serve hot

Variations:

- Feel free to mix and match varieties of mushrooms, if desired. While this is a great basic recipe, it also works well with more exotic mushrooms swapped in. Play around with your favourites!

- For a vegetarian version, swap out the chicken broth for vegetable broth.

Cream of Mushroom Soup

Mac and Cheese

In my experience, when it comes to making macaroni and cheese ... using store bought, dried pasta is best. Not only is it fast, easy, and cheap, it's also a bit more robust, able to take the extra handling that comes with stirring cheese sauce into it, etc.

When it comes to gluten-free mac and cheese, the same still holds, even if the boxed stuff isn't as dirt cheap as regular pasta. Use whatever brand and shape of pasta you like, just use a gentle hand when it comes to stirring it. If the pasta falls apart... well, it still tastes awesome, right? Personally, I like using a shape like fusilli or rotini, as I just find it more fun to eat. Additionally, I find that brown rice pasta tends to hold its shape better than other varieties of gf pasta.

Dry gluten free pasta	12 oz	375 g
Butter	1/4 cup	50 ml
White rice flour	1/4 cup	50 ml
Dijon mustard	2 Tbsp	30 ml
Garlic cloves, crushed	2	2
Dry white wine	1 cup	250 ml
Milk	2 cups	500 ml
Salt	1 tsp	5 ml
Shredded gouda cheese	8 oz	250 g
Shredded provolone cheese	8 oz	250 g
Shredded cheddar cheese	8 oz	250 g
Pepper		
Gluten-free cracker crumbs	1 cup	250 ml

Preheat oven to 350 degrees F. Grease large glass baking dish with butter, shortening, or pan spray.

Cook pasta to "al dente" firmness - tender enough to eat, but not soft-soft. It will continue to cook after adding the cheese. Rinse with cold water, drain well. Set aside.

In a large saucepan, melt butter over medium-high heat. Add rice flour, whisk well. Cook for two minutes, whisking constantly. Add Dijon mustard, garlic, and white wine, whisk until smooth. Add milk and salt, stir well. Bring just to a simmer.

Set aside about 1 cup of the shredded cheese, for the top of the casserole. Add the remaining cheese to the pot 1 handful at a time, stirring to melt/combine. Once all of the cheese is incorporated and the sauce is smooth and silky, gently fold in prepared pasta before pouring into greased baking dish. Top with reserved cheese and cracker crumbs if desired.

Bake for 30 minutes, or until top is golden brown and bubbly. Serve hot.

Variations:

- Add 1/2 - 1 lb (250-500g) cooked, crumbled bacon to the cheese sauce, just before adding pasta

- Add florets of cauliflower and/or broccoli. Steamed or roasted works best.

- Substitute milk for the wine of desired

- Substitute types of cheese. While this is my favourite combo, have fun with it. Try a bit of smoked cheddar, or substitute Gruyere for the cheddar. Hot pepper cheese? Why not?

Mac and Cheese

Gnocchi

When making gnocchi, technique really matters. You don't want the potatoes to get too waterlogged when boiling, or you'll end up with very heavy, doughy gnocchi. At every stage of mixing the potatoes, you want to use a light hand - try to keep the mixture fluffy and relatively loose, up until the point that you're rolling them. Handling everything gently will ensure that you'll end up with soft, pillowy gnocchi.

Makes 4-6 servings

Russet potatoes	3 lbs	1500 g
White rice flour	1 cup	250 ml
Light buckwheat flour	1/2 cup	125 ml
Sweet rice flour	1/2 cup	125 ml
Amaranth flour	1/4 cup	50 ml
Large eggs, beaten	3	3
Potato starch for rolling		
Salt		

Cut potatoes into halves, place in a large pot of boiling water. Cook until tender, but not falling apart - about 35-45 minutes. Strain well, set aside to cool slightly. Once potatoes are just cool enough to handle, peel skin off them and mash or put through a ricer - make sure there are no lumps. Set aside to cool completely.

In a separate bowl, whisk together flours to combine well. Add flour mixture to cooled potato, gentle fold to combine. Add eggs, once again gently folding to combine. Cover tightly with plastic film, allow to rest for about 15 minutes.

Generously dust your work surface with potato starch. Dump gnocchi dough out, knead gently to bring together into a soft ball. If the dough is sticky, add a little potato starch until it's workable. Divide dough into 8-10 roughly equal pieces. One at a time, roll each out into long "snakes", each about the thickness of a thumb. Cut each roll into bite-sized pieces, about 3/4"-1" long.

If you're feeling lazy, you can cook these up as-is. Otherwise, you can roll them over a fork to produce the traditional ridged gnocchi shape. There are many possible ways to do this, and you may want to play with it a bit until you find your own groove. For me, I gently (but firmly!) roll each gnocchi over the back of the fork, aiming towards the pointed ends of the tines. As I roll, the gnocchi will curl over itself into a slight "c" shape. Practice, experiment, and if necessary - Youtube has great tutorials for a variety of methods.

Start a fresh pot of boiling water (or reuse your potato water, if you so choose!), and salt it well. Bring it to a gentle, not rolling boil, and cook your gnocchi in batches. As they float to the top, allow them to cook another 30 seconds or so before using a slotted spoon to remove them, transferring to a clean bowl or plate. Serve hot and fresh, with sauce of your choice - we prefer pesto, as pictured.

Gnocchi in Pesto

Thin Crust Pizza

Pizza

We made SO MUCH pizza in preparation for the book. Having gotten pretty good at winging dough recipes by that point, we had a lot of really good pizza - there are so many different ways to do pizza. Thin crust, thick crust, "deep dish", etc. In the end, I settled on two great basic recipes.

Both hold up well, making pizza slices that you can actually pick up and eat, like a regular pizza. Both taste better than even higher quality frozen pizzas - even full gluten ones.

The deep dish uses oil in the pan to create the crispy "fried" texture that we loved from one of the local (gluten!) pizza places, while the thin crust is crisp and crunchy, without the weird flavours and textures normally associated with thin crust gluten-free pizzas.

Thin Crust Pizza

Makes two 12" pizzas

Warm water	1 1/2 cups	375 ml
Liquid honey	2 Tbsp	30 ml
Salt	2 tsp	10 ml
Active dry yeast	1 Tbsp	15 ml
Brown rice flour	1 1/4 cups	300 ml
Light buckwheat flour	3/4 cup	175 ml
White rice flour	3/4 cup	175 ml
Potato starch (plus extra for rolling)	1/2 cup	125 ml
Tapioca starch	1 Tbsp	15 ml
Xanthan gum	2 tsp	10 ml
Olive oil	1/4 cup	50 ml
Extra Olive oil		

Sauce
Toppings
Cheese

Add honey and salt to warm water, stir till well blended. Add yeast and stir again. Allow to sit (somewhere warm!) for 10 minutes.

In the bowl of a stand mixer, combine flours, starches, and xanthan gum. Add olive oil, mixing until evenly distributed. Add yeast mixture, mix well. Dough should ball up a bit, but be a bit sticky. Cover loosely with plastic wrap, allow to rise in a warm area for 1 hour.

Preheat oven to 425 F (220 C). Line pizza pans with parchment paper, if they're not nonstick.

Generously dust work surface with potato starch. Divide dough into two equal sized portions. Roll each dough piece out to form 12" diameter pizza crusts, generously dusting the tops of the dough with additional potato starch, as needed. Transfer to pizza pans.

Using a pastry brush, spread a very thin coat of olive oil over the entire top side of each crust. Bake for 10 minutes.

Remove crusts from the oven. Spread sauce over prepared pizza crust. Scatter toppings across the pizza, top with shredded cheese. Bake for another 10-15 minutes, or until cheese is bubbly and starting to brown. Serve hot.

Deep Dish Pizza

Makes one 12" round or 12 x 9" rectangle pizza

Warm water	1 1/2 cups	375 ml
Liquid honey	2 Tbsp	30 ml
Salt	2 tsp	10 ml
Active dry yeast	4 1/2 tsp	22 ml
Brown rice flour	1 1/4 cups	300 ml
Gluten-free oat flour	3/4 cup	175 ml
Millet flour	1/2 cup	125 ml
Cornstarch	1/2 cup	125 ml
Potato starch	1/3 cup	75 ml
Xanthan gum	3 tsp	15 ml
Olive oil	1/4 cup	50 ml
Extra Olive oil		

Sauce
Toppings
Cheese

Add honey and salt to warm water, stir till well blended. Add yeast and stir again. Allow to sit (somewhere warm!) for 10 minutes.

In the bowl of a stand mixer, combine flours, starches, and xanthan gum. Add olive oil, mixing until evenly distributed. Add yeast mixture, mix well. Dough should ball up a bit, but be a bit sticky.

Grease the bottom and sides of a 12" round pizza pan (or, what we used – a 9 x 13" baking pan). Press the dough evenly throughout the bottom pan, with a bit pushed up around the sides as an outer crust. Cover loosely with plastic wrap, allow to rise in a warm area for 1 hour.

Preheat oven to 500 F (260 C)

Using a pastry brush, spread a very thin coat of olive oil over the entire top side of the crust. Bake for 5 minutes. Remove crust from the oven. Spread sauce over prepared pizza crust. Scatter toppings across the pizza, top with shredded cheese. Bake for another 15 minutes.

Calzones

Of all the recipes that he's loved from the development of this book, this is the one that my husband has become the most fanatical about - completely obsessed would be an understatement. Although he's not gluten-free himself, he'd happily live on these, declaring them to be the best calzones he's ever had!

These are best started about a day before serving, due to the rise and chill times. I promise it's worth the effort. The crust holds together well - as it really needs to for a proper calzone - and the flour combination is delicious. Flavourful, works well with traditional pizza fillings, without clashing or overpowering them.

Makes 4 Large Calzones

Brown rice flour	1 1/4 cup	300 ml
Gluten-free oat flour	3/4 cup	175 ml
Amaranth flour	1/2 cup	125 ml
Millet flour	1/2 cup	125 ml
Corn starch	1/2 cup	125 ml
Potato starch	1/3 cup	75 ml
Tapioca starch	2 Tbsp	30 ml
Xanthan gum	3 tsp	15 ml
Liquid honey	1 Tbsp	15 ml
Warm water, divided	1 1/2 cup	375 ml
Active dry yeast	4 tsp	20 ml
Salt	2 tsp	10 ml
Olive oil	1/4 cup	50 ml
Large egg	1	1
Additional potato starch for rolling		
Pizza fillings of choice: cheese, meats, peppers, mushrooms, etc.		
Large egg	1	1
Tbsp water	1	1

Whisk flours, starches, and xanthan gum together until well combined. Set aside.

Add honey to 1 1/4 cup warm water, stir till well blended. Add yeast and stir again. Allow to sit (somewhere warm!) for 10 minutes.

Divide flour mix roughly in half. In a large bowl, combine half of the flour mix with the yeast and water mixture, mixing well to combine. Cover loosely with plastic wrap, allow to rise in a warm area for 1 hour.

Once the hour is complete, add remaining flour, salt, remaining water, olive oil, and egg, mixing well to combine. Cover loosely with plastic wrap, allow to rise in a warm area for 1 more hour.

Once second rise is complete, knead dough, wrap tightly in plastic, and chill for at least 12 hours.

1 hour before baking calzones, remove dough from the fridge. Loosen plastic wrap slightly, divide dough into 4 equal sized balls, and allow to rise in a warm area for 1 hour.

Preheat oven to 400 F (200 C), line two baking sheets with parchment paper.

Generously dust work surface with potato starch. Roll each of the 4 dough balls into a rough that's about 8-9" across. One at a time, carefully transfer dough to a prepared baking sheet. Arrange pizza fillings of your choice on one half of the round, allowing approximately 1" worth of border around the edge. Whisk egg and water together, brush along edge of dough. Fold uncovered half of dough over the fillings, press to seal edge - we used a fork. Repeat for remaining dough balls.

Brush tops of calzones with egg wash, prick the tops a few times with a fork, bake for 15 minutes or until golden brown. Serve hot.

Calzones

Double Chocolate Brownies

Desserts

Double Chocolate Brownies

You may have gathered by now: I'm kind of opinionated. Ok, more than kind of – REALLY opinionated. When it comes to brownies, it's no different. There's a lot of stuff out there that passes itself off as "brownie", when it's just… not. Let me preach for a moment…

You see, brownies aren't cake. They're not supposed to be cake. I'm not even big on chocolate, but am constantly disappointed when "brownie" ends up being just sort of a chocolate cake. Brownies should be relatively thin, rich, moist, and gooey. GOOEY IS A REQUIREMENT. Leavening ingredients don't belong in a proper brownie recipe. Disagree? Too bad, this is my book!

Brownies are about the easiest baked good you can make – you don't even need a mixer, just stir the ingredients together in a bowl and you're done. No whipping, creaming… nothing. Stir it, dump it in a pan and bake it. Done. Love it.

This recipe makes a 9 x 13" pan worth of chocolate, gooey, awesome brownies.

Cocoa	1 cup	250 ml
Granulated sugar	1 cup	250 ml
Light brown sugar, packed	1 cup	250 ml
Light buckwheat flour	1/2 cup	125 ml
Sorghum flour	1/4 cup	50 ml
Coconut flour	1/4 cup	50 ml
Salt	1/2 tsp	2 ml
Large eggs, beaten	4	4
Butter, melted	1 cup	250 ml
Chocolate chunks	1 cup	250 ml
Chocolate chips*	1 cup	250 ml

Preheat oven to 350 F (180 C). Prepare 9 x 13 pan (or two 8 x 8" pans) with pan spray or shortening.

In large mixing bowl, combine dry ingredients ingredients. Add beaten eggs and melted butter, stir until dry ingredients are well incorporated and wet. Add chocolate chunks and walnuts, stir until evenly distributed in the batter.

Spread batter into prepared pan(s), Bake for 20 – 25 minutes for 8 x 8" pans, or 30-35 minutes for 9 x 13" pan. Brownies are done when knife inserted into center comes out clean. Let cool completely before cutting into squares. Enjoy!

* If you'd like to have some fun with your brownie, substitute 1 cup of walnuts, almonds, or… whatever. M & Ms. Reese's Pieces. Andes Mint Chips. Whatever will make you happy!

Blondies

As someone who's not a huge fan of chocolate, I love blondies. They give you the same satisfaction as a good brownie, but sans chocolate. Perfect.

This recipe is great on its own, as a basic, butterscotchy bar... but they really sing with the addition of a few spices, as a chai blondie!

Dark brown sugar, packed	1 cup	250 ml
Granulated Sugar	1 cup	250 ml
Baking powder	1 tsp	5 ml
Salt	Pinch	pinch
Sorghum flour	1 cup	250 ml
Light buckwheat flour	1/2 cup	125 ml
Millet flour	1/2 cup	125 ml
Tapioca starch	1 Tbsp	15 ml
Large eggs, beaten	4	4
Butter, melted	1 cup	250 ml
Vanilla extract	1 tsp	5 ml

Preheat oven to 350 F (180 C). Prepare 9 x 13 pan (or two 8 x 8" pans) with pan spray or shortening.

In large mixing bowl, combine all of the dry ingredients. Add beaten eggs, melted butter, and vanilla extract, stir until dry ingredients are well incorporated.

Spread batter into prepared pan(s), Bake for 20 – 25 minutes for 8 x 8" pans, or 30-35 minutes for 9 x 13" pan.

Blondies are done when knife inserted into center comes out clean. Let cool completely before cutting into squares.

Chai variation: Add 2 Tbsp (30 ml) instant tea, 1 tsp (5 ml) each cinnamon and cardamom, and 1/2 tsp (2 ml) each cloves and nutmeg to the dry ingredients

Blondies

159

Chewy Lemon Bars

I love these bars - they have the gooey texture of a proper brownie, but are lemony instead of chocolatey. Quick and easy to make, also!

Butter, room temperature	1/2 cup	125 ml
Granulated sugar	1 cup	250 ml
Large eggs	3	3
Juice of one lemon		
Zest from two lemons		
Light buckwheat flour	1/4 cup	50 ml
Sorghum flour	1/4 cup	50 ml
Sweet rice flour	1/4 cup	50 ml
Coconut flour	1/4 cup	50 ml
Baking powder	1/2 tsp	2 ml
Xanthan gum	1/2 tsp	2 ml
Salt	1/2 tsp	2 ml

Glaze:

Icing (powdered) sugar	2 cups	500 ml
Juice of one lemon		
Salt	pinch	pinch

Preheat oven to 350F (180C). Grease an 8"x 8" square cake pan with vegetable shortening or baking spray.

Cream together butter and sugar until pale and fluffy. Add eggs, lemon juice and lemon zest, continue to beat until well incorporated and smooth.

In a separate bowl, whisk together flours, baking powder, xanthan gum and salt. Add this dry mix to the wet ingredients, stir gently until everything is well distributed.

Transfer batter to prepared baking pan, spreading evenly. Bake for 20-25 minutes, or until set in the middle. Do not over cook!

Allow bars to cool completely, before making the glaze:

Whisk together lemon juice, salt, and icing sugar until smooth. Spread desired amount over cooled bars, allow to set up before slicing and serving.

Chewy Lemon Bars

Raspberry Coconut Bars

When I was a kid, my grandmother made the most fabulous raspberry coconut bars. They were a cookie base that wasn't super sweet - almost like a shortbread - topped with raspberry jam and a coconut mixture that was crispy on top and chewy underneath... incredibly addictive.

This is my gluten-free version of her recipe.

Butter, softened	3/4 cup	175 ml
Granulated sugar	2 Tbsp	30 ml
Large eggs	2	2
Milk	1 Tbsp	15 ml
Vanilla	1 tsp	5 ml
Sorghum flour	1/2 cup	125 ml
Brown rice flour	1/2 cup	125 ml
Coconut flour	1/4 cup	50 ml
Tapioca starch	1 Tbsp	15 ml
Xanthan gum	1 tsp	5 ml
Baking powder	1 tsp	5 ml
Salt	1/2 tsp	2 ml
Raspberry preserves	3/4 cup	175 ml
Large eggs	2	2
Granulated sugar	1 1/2 cup	375 ml
Shredded coconut	3 cups	750 ml
Butter, melted	3 Tbsp	45 ml
Vanilla.	1 tsp	5 ml

In stand mixer, cream butter and sugar until fluffy. Add eggs, milk, and vanilla, beat until everything is fully incorporated and smooth.

In a large bowl, mix together flours, starch, xanthan gum, baking powder, and salt. Slowly add this dry mix to the mixer bowl, and carefully mix until well incorporated and smooth. Wrap dough in plastic film, chill for 1 hour.

Preheat the oven to 350 F (180 C), Grease bottom and sides of 9 x 13" pan with shortening or pan spray.

Spread dough over bottom of pant, pressing to form a crust of relatively even thickness. Spread raspberry preserves evenly over the crust.

Whisk eggs until foamy. Add sugar, whisk until well combined. Add remaining ingredients, stir to combine well. Drop spoonfuls of the coconut mixture all over the raspberry layer, and gently spread to create a solid layer.

Bake 30-40 minutes until golden brown. Cool to almost room temperature before cutting into squares, allow to fully cool before lifting from pan and serving.

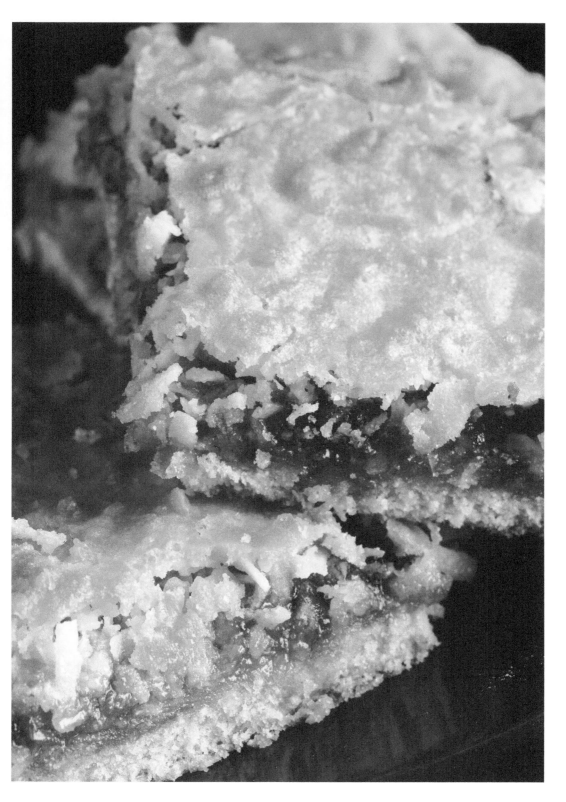

Raspberry Coconut Bars

Chewy Chocolate Chip Cookies

When developing this recipe, I ran into a unique cookbook issue: They tasted SO good as raw batter, they almost didn't get baked into actual cookies!

These cookies are a stellar example of what can happen with you really hit the right combination of alternative flours, to come up with something even tastier than the original, full-gluten version. Hit the right combination, in the right proportions... And WOW. I may never make wheat-flour chocolate chip cookies ever again ... even for non-GF friends!

Want to use this recipe for raw cookie dough, either to add to ice cream, or to enjoy straight from the bowl (I don't judge!)? Use pasteurized eggs!

Makes about 30 cookies

Butter, softened	1 cup	250 ml
Dark brown sugar, packed	1 cup	250 ml
Granulated sugar	1/2 cup	125 ml
Large eggs	2	2
Milk	1 Tbsp	15 ml
Vanilla extract	2 tsp	10 ml
Brown rice flour	1 cup	250 ml
Sorghum flour	1 cup	250 ml
Coconut flour	1/4 cup	50 ml
Tapioca starch	2 Tbsp	30 ml
Xanthan gum	1 tsp	5 ml
Salt	1 tsp	5 ml
Baking soda	1 tsp	5 ml
Baking powder	1/2 tsp	2 ml
1 bag milk chocolate chips	~ 2 cups	~ 500 ml

In stand mixer, cream butter and sugar until fluffy. Add eggs, milk, and vanilla, beat until everything is fully incorporated and smooth.

In a large bowl, mix together remaining ingredients. Slowly add this dry mix to the mixer bowl, and carefully mix until well incorporated and smooth. Chill dough for 1 hour.

Preheat the oven to 375F (190 C), line baking sheets with parchment paper.

Roll 1" balls out of the cookie dough. Arrange dough balls on baking sheets leaving at least 2" between cookies - they flatten out a fair amount. Gently press the tops of each slightly - flatten JUST enough to prevent the dough from rolling.

Bake for 11-13 minutes. Cookies will look puffy, but flatten out as they cool. Do not overbake!

Chewy Chocolate Chip Cookies

Chewy Chocolate Cookies

These cookies are everything you could ever want in a cookie... chewy, fudgy, dense, and full of flavour. Add whatever "stuff" you'd like - nuts, chocolate chips, dried fruit, caramels - to create your personalized perfect chocolate cookie.

Butter, softened	1 cup	250 ml
Dark brown sugar, packed	1 cup	250 ml
Granulated sugar	1/2 cup	125 ml
Large eggs	3	3
Milk	1 Tbsp	15 ml
Vanilla extract	2 tsp	10 ml
Brown rice flour	1/2 cup	125 ml
Sorghum flour	3/4 cup	175 ml
Coconut flour	1/4 cup	50 ml
Cocoa	3/4 cup	175 ml
Tapioca starch	2 Tbsp	30 ml
Xanthan gum	1 tsp	5 ml
Salt	1 tsp	5 ml
Baking soda	1 tsp	5 ml
Baking powder	1/2 tsp	2 ml
"Stuff": chocolate chips, nuts, etc	2 cups	500 ml

In stand mixer, cream butter and sugars until fluffy. Add eggs, milk, and vanilla, beat until everything is fully incorporated and smooth.

In a large bowl, mix together remaining ingredients. Slowly add this dry mix to the mixer bowl, and carefully mix until well incorporated and smooth. Chill dough for 1 hour.

Preheat the oven to 375 F (190 C) , line baking sheets with parchment paper.

Roll 1" balls out of the cookie dough. Arrange dough balls on baking sheets leaving at least 2" between cookies - they flatten out a fair amount. Gently press the tops of each slightly - flatten JUST enough to prevent the dough from rolling.

Bake for 11-13 minutes. Cookies will look puffy, but flatten out as they cool. Do not over bake!

Sea Salt and Caramel variation, as pictured:

Use caramel baking pieces if available, or cut soft caramel squares into small pieces to use as "stuff". As soon as cookies are finished baking, lightly sprinkle tops with coarse sea salt, press lightly into top of cookies.

Chewy Chocolate Cookies

Chewy Ginger-Molasses Cookies

Growing up, my grandmother made fabulous chewy ginger cookies. We always called them "Ginger snaps", and it wasn't til I was an adult that I realized that was actually incorrect. Oh well, I've never been one for the crispier version of these cookies - I love the soft, chewy version! This was one of the very first recipes I decided to make over as a gluten-free version.

Butter, softened	3/4 cup	175 ml
Granulated sugar	1 cup	250 ml
Molasses	1/2 cup	125 ml
Large eggs	2	2
Vanilla extract	2 tsp	10 ml
Brown rice flour	1 cup	250 ml
Sorghum flour	1 cup	250 ml
Coconut flour	1/4 cup	50 ml
Tapioca starch	2 Tbsp	30 ml
Xanthan gum	1 tsp	5 ml
Baking soda	1 1/2 tsp	7 ml
Baking powder	1/2 tsp	2 ml
Salt	1 tsp	5 ml
Ginger powder	1 tsp	5 ml
Cinnamon	1 tsp	5 ml
Ground cloves	1 tsp	5 ml
Additional sugar for dipping		

In stand mixer, cream butter and sugar until fluffy. Add molasses and egg, beat until everything is fully incorporated and smooth.

In a large bowl, mix together remaining ingredients. Slowly add this dry mix to the mixer bowl, and carefully mix until well incorporated and smooth. Chill dough for 1 hour.

Preheat the oven to 350 F (180 C).

Roll 1" balls out of the cookie dough, dip 1 side into sugar, and place sugar side up on a greased cookie sheet, leaving at least 2" between cookies - they flatten out a fair amount.

Bake for 10-12 minutes. Cookies will look puffy, but flatten out as they cool. Do not over bake!

Chewy Ginger-Molasses Cookies

Shortbread

While milk is not a traditional ingredient in shortbread, I use it to soften the flours for a better final texture in this recipe.

Makes about 15 3" cookies

Butter, softened	3/4 cup	175 ml
Light brown sugar, packed	1/2 cup	125 ml
Milk	2 Tbsp	30 ml
Vanilla extract	1 tsp	5 ml
White rice flour	1/2 cup	125 ml
Sorghum flour	1/2 cup	125 ml
Coconut flour	1/4 cup	50 ml
Corn starch	1/4 cup	50 ml
Tapioca starch	1 Tbsp	15 ml
Xanthan gum	1 tsp	5 ml
Salt	1/4 tsp	1 ml
Corn starch, for rolling		

Mix butter and brown sugar together just until combined - do not cream it or over beat it. Add milk and vanilla, gently mix until combined

In a separate bowl, whisk together remaining ingredients. Add dry mix to butter and sugar, mix until combined. Knead until smooth. Wrap dough in plastic film, chill for 1 hour.

Preheat the oven to 350 F (180 C), line baking sheets with parchment paper.

Generously sprinkle clean work surface with corn starch, roll dough to 1/2" thick. Cut into traditional rectangles, or use cookie cutters to cut out whatever shapes you'd like. Place cookies 2" apart on prepared baking sheets.

Bake for about 15 minutes, or until lightly golden. Allow cookies to cool on cookie sheets for at least 5 minutes before moving, cool completely before serving.

Shortbread

Rolled Sugar Cookies for Decorating

This is a great basic recipe for rolled sugar cookies. It is easy to make, rolls out beautifully, spreads minimally when baking, and tastes delicious!

Makes about 20 3" cookies

Brown rice flour	1 cup	250 ml
Sorghum flour	1 cup	250 ml
Coconut flour	1/4 cup	50 ml
Tapioca starch	2 Tbsp	30 ml
Xanthan gum	2 tsp	10 ml
Baking powder	1 tsp	5 ml
Salt	1/2 tsp	2 ml
Butter, softened	3/4 cup	175 ml
Granulated sugar	1 1/4 cup	300 ml
Large eggs	2	2
Vanilla extract	1 tsp	5 ml
corn starch, for rolling		

Royal icing recipe (Page 175)

Whisk together all dry ingredients (except sugar and corn starch) until well combined, set aside.

In a stand mixer, cream together butter and sugar until smooth and fluffy. Add in eggs, one at a time, beating well between each addition. Add vanilla extract, and mix until well incorporated and smooth.

Slowly add dry mix to the mixer bowl, and carefully mix until well incorporated and smooth. Wrap dough in plastic film, chill for 1 hour.

Preheat oven to 400 F (200 C), line cookie sheets with parchment paper

Generously sprinkle clean work surface with corn starch, roll dough to 1/4" thick (can be slightly thicker). Use cookie cutters to cut out whatever shapes you'd like, place cookies 2" apart on greased cookie sheets.

Bake cookies for 8-10 minutes, or until bottoms look lightly golden. Allow cookies to cool on cookie sheets for at least 5 minutes before moving. Cookies need to cool completely before decorating. Decorate with Royal Icing, page 175

Decorated Sugar Cookies

173

Gingerbread Cookies

Gingerbread cookies are one of the most iconic foodstuffs from the holiday season. Now, it's one of the easiest ways to feel included in the festivities, for those that are gluten free. Rolled out to 1/4" or slightly thicker, this recipe makes for a thick, soft cookie. If you prefer your gingerbread to be crispy, roll them out slightly thinner than 1/4".

These are great on their own, but look even more festive with the addition of piped royal icing accents. For more colour, use the frosting as "glue" to secure various candies to your gingerbread people!

Makes about 30 3 1/2" cookies

Butter, softened	1/2 cup	125 ml
Dark brown sugar, packed	3/4 cup	175 ml
Large eggs	2	2
Molasses	1/2 cup	125 ml
Vanilla	1 Tbsp	15 ml
Brown rice flour	1 1/4 cup	300 ml
Sorghum flour	1 1/4 cup	300 ml
Coconut flour	1/3 cup	75 ml
Tapioca starch	1/4 cup	50 ml
Corn starch	1/4 cup	50 ml
Xanthan gum	2 tsp	10 ml
Baking powder	1 1/2 tsp	7 ml
Baking soda	3/4 tsp	3 ml
Salt	1/2 tsp	2 ml
Ground ginger	1 Tbsp	15 ml
Cinnamon	2 tsp	10 ml
Ground cloves	1/4 tsp	1 ml
Corn starch, for rolling		
Royal icing, for decorating		

In stand mixer, cream butter and sugar until fluffy. Add eggs, molasses, and vanilla, mix on low speed until everything is fully incorporated and smooth.

In a large bowl, mix together remaining ingredients. Slowly add this dry mix to the mixer bowl, and carefully mix until well incorporated and smooth. Chill dough for 1 hour.

Preheat the oven to 375 F (190 C), line baking sheets with parchment paper.

Generously sprinkle clean work surface with corn starch, roll dough to 1/4" thick (can be slightly thicker). Use cookie cutters to cut out whatever shapes you'd like, place cookies 2" apart on prepared baking sheets. Bake 7-10 minutes. Cookies will look puffy, but flatten out a little as they cool. Don't over bake if you want them soft! Allow cookies to cool completely before decorating with royal icing.

Royal Icing

Large egg whites	4	4
lemon juice	1 Tbsp	15 ml
Icing (powdered) sugar	4-6 cups	1000-1500 ml

In clean stand mixer, whip egg whites until foamy. Add lemon juice, whip for another minute. Slowly add powdered sugar until cookie icing reaches desired consistency. You will want a fairly thick frosting – but still smooth and workable – for piping details and borders.

A good way to figure out if your frosting is the right consistency is to pull a spoon through the middle of the frosting bowl.

If the frosting settles out in less than 5 seconds, it's too runny. Add a little more powdered sugar. If the frosting settles out in 5-10 seconds, you're good to go!
 If the frosting takes longer than 10 seconds to settle, it's too thick. Add a little water or lemon juice and try again.

Cover the frosting tightly with plastic wrap when not in use. Have the wrap sitting right on the surface with NO air pockets, vent holes, etc. The frosting dries out FAST.

175

Pecan Pie Cookies

The wheat version of these cookies been one of - and much of the time *THE* - most popular recipes on my blog, ever since I first posted it. As a gluten-free cookie, these definitely do not disappoint: The various alternative flours bring a complexity to the base cookie that just isn't there in the all-purpose flour recipe.

Makes about 24 large cookies

Butter, softened	3/4 cup	175 ml
Light brown sugar, packed	1 cup	250 ml
Large egg	1	1
Vanilla	1 tsp	5 ml
Sorghum flour	1/2 cup	125 ml
White rice flour	1 cup	250 ml
Brown rice flour	1/4 cup	50 ml
Corn starch	1/4 cup	50 ml
Tapioca starch	1/4 cup	50 ml
Xanthan gum	2 tsp	10 ml
Baking powder	1 tsp	5 ml
Salt	1/2 tsp	2 ml
Chopped pecans	1 cup	250 ml
Light brown sugar, packed	1/2 cup	125 ml
Heavy whipping cream	1/4 cup	50 ml
Vanilla	1 tsp	5 ml

Pinch each of ginger, cinnamon, and cloves

Cream butter and sugar until light and fluffy. Add egg and vanilla, continue beating until egg is fully incorporated and mixture is once again smooth and fluffy.

In a large bowl, mix together flours, starches, xanthan gum, baking powder, and salt. Slowly add this dry mix to the mixer bowl, and carefully mix until well incorporated and smooth. Wrap dough in plastic film, chill for 1 hour.

Preheat oven to 350 F (180 C). Line 2 cookie sheets with parchment paper.

In a separate mixing bowl, mix pecans, brown sugar and spices. Add in heavy cream and vanilla, mix until well combined.

Roll cookie dough into balls that are about 1.5" in diameter, and place them on cookie sheets – leave about 2" between the cookies. Gently use thumb to press down in the middle of each cookie, making an indentation. Roll thumb slightly to stretch the indentation out a little. Fill each indentation with about 1 tsp of pecan filling

Bake for 12-14 minutes, until lightly browned. Allow to cool on sheets for 5 minutes or so, before gently transferring to baking rack or counter to finish cooling.

Pecan Pie Cookies

Carrot Cake Cookies

Carrot Cake Cookies

These cookies really morphed from the time I decided to do a carrot cake cookie, and what ended up as the final product. The very first version turned out so horribly, I almost didn't continue to pursue the idea! No flavour, horrible texture... really bad. It was a rare, upsetting occurrence for me!

The second - and final - version cut out the pineapple, and went from being just a basic dropped cookie, to being sandwich cookies. Carrot cake needs cream cheese frosting, and the cookies needed the same - accented with both maple syrup and orange zest.

These are insane. Chewy cookie packed with flavour, perfectly complimented with the filling. The cookies themselves are actually pretty healthy (if you skip the filling!), and hold their own as a quick snack.

Makes 12-15 sandwich cookies

Butter, softened	1/2 cup	125 ml
Light brown sugar, packed	1/2 cup	125 ml
Granulated sugar	1/2 cup	125 ml
Large eggs	2	2
Vanilla	1 tsp	5 ml
Zest of one orange, divided		
Brown rice flour	3/4 cup	175 ml
Sorghum flour	1/2 cup	125 ml
Coconut flour	1/4 cup	50 ml
Tapioca starch	1 Tbsp	15 ml
Cinnamon	1 1/2 tsp	7 ml
Xanthan gum	1 tsp	5 ml
Nutmeg	1/2 tsp	2 ml
Cloves	1/4 tsp	1 ml
Baking powder	1/2 tsp	2 ml
Baking soda	1/4 tsp	1 ml
Salt	3/4 tsp	3 ml
Grated carrots	1 cup	250 ml
Walnuts, chopped	1/2 cup	125 ml
Raisins	1 cup	250 ml

Filling:

Cream cheese, softened	8 oz	250 g
Maple syrup	1 Tbsp	15 ml
Salt	pinch	pinch
Icing (powdered) sugar	2 cups	500 ml

In stand mixer, cream butter and sugars until fluffy. Add eggs, vanilla, and half of the orange zest, beat until everything is fully incorporated and smooth.

In a large bowl, mix together Flours, starch, spices, xanthan gum, baking powder, baking soda and salt. Slowly add this dry mix to the mixer bowl, and carefully mix until well incorporated and smooth. Add carrots, walnuts and raisins, continue mixing until uniformly combined. Wrap dough in plastic film, chill for 1 hour.

Preheat the oven to 375 F (190 C), line baking sheets with parchment paper.

Roll 1" balls out of the cookie dough. Arrange dough balls on baking sheets leaving at least 2" between cookies - they flatten out a fair amount. Gently press the tops of each slightly - flatten JUST enough to prevent the dough from rolling.

Use a tablespoon, cookie scoop, or small ice cream scoop to drop rounded spoonfuls of the batter onto prepared baking sheets. Use a moistened spoon to slightly flatten cookies. Bake for about 15 minutes, until golden brown. Remove cookies from oven, use a spatula to gently flatten them - this will make them easier to eat! Allow to cool on sheets for 5 minutes or so, before gently transferring to baking racks to finish cooling.

Once cookies are cool, pair cookies into sets of 2 that are similar in size/shape. Scoop a bit of filling onto one cookie, sandwich with the remaining cookie. Repeat for all remaining pairs of cookies.

Whisk together cream cheese, maple syrup, salt, and remaining orange zest. Slowly add powdered sugar until cookie filling reaches desired consistency. You'll want it very thick, but still spreadable.

Fig Newtons

This recipe takes a bit of doing - the filling needs to be made and cooled, the dough needs to be chilled - but the result is well worth the time and effort. This produces a fragrant, delicious cookie that is sure to satisfy your comfort food cravings.

Butter, softened	1/2 cup	125 ml
Granulated sugar	1/4 cup	50 ml
Brown sugar, packed	1/4 cup	50 ml
Large egg	1	1
Orange juice	1 Tbsp	15 ml
Vanilla extract	1 tsp	5 ml
Zest of 1/2 orange		
White rice flour	1/2 cup	125 ml
Sorghum flour	1/2 cup	125 ml
Coconut flour	1/4 cup	50 ml
Millet flour	1/4 cup	50 ml
Tapioca starch	1 Tbsp	15 ml
Xanthan gum	1 tsp	5 ml
Salt	1/2 tsp	2 ml
Baking powder	1/2 tsp	2 ml

Filling:

Dried mission figs	12 oz	375 g
Water	1/3 cup	75 ml
Zest of 1/2 orange		
Salt	pinch	pinch

Corn starch, for rolling

In stand mixer, cream butter and sugars until fluffy. Add egg, orange juice, vanilla, and orange zest, beat until everything is fully incorporated and smooth.

In a large bowl, mix together remaining ingredients. Slowly add this dry mix to the mixer bowl, and carefully mix until well incorporated and smooth. Chill dough for 1 hour.

To make the filling:

Remove any stems from the dried figs, discard. Finely chop figs. Place into a saucepan with water, bring to a moil over medium-high heat. Once mixture starts to boil, cover and remove from heat. Allow to sit for 10 minutes, or until all of the water is absorbed by the figs.

Transfer fig mixture to food processor, along with orange zest and salt. Process until very smooth. Transfer to a clean bowl, loosely cover with plastic film, and allow to cool to room temperature.

To Assemble:

Preheat the oven to 375 F (190 C), line baking sheets with parchment paper.

Divide dough into 4 equal balls. Generously sprinkle clean work surface with corn starch. Roll one dough ball into a long, thin, and narrow strip - about 4" x 12". Trim to square up / tidy the edges.

Stir cooled fig mixture to incorporate any condensation that has developed. Transfer about one quarter of the filling to a pastry bag, or heavyweight plastic bag with a corner cut off - either way, you'll want about 1/2" diameter opening.

Pipe a long, fat line of filling up the center of the rolled dough, using up all of the filling in the bag. Use a clean spoon to gently spread the filling to a width of slightly more than 1".

Gently fold one long side of dough over the filling. Fold the other long side over that, forming a long tube of filled cookie. Gently flip over, slice into cookies (About 1.5" long pieces), and gently transfer to prepared baking sheet.

Repeat with remaining dough and filling.

Bake for 12-15 minutes, or until edges are just starting to turn golden brown. Do not over bake!

Remove cookies from baking sheet, immediately cover with plastic wrap or - as we do - a long cake pan. Allow to steam/cool like this for at least 30 minutes. While these CAN be eaten right away, it's best to let them sit overnight to let the moisture levels of the filling / cookie balance out a bit.

Fig Newtons

Noelles

Unlike most of my recipes - which are created completely from scratch - this one actually has quite the lineage to it. This is the gluten-free version of my regular Noelles... which is a more adult (Amaretto!) version of my aunt's famous Christmas cookies recipe, which I grew up looking forward to every year. From what I can tell, HER recipe was an adaptation of a recipe from a chocolate chip cookies ad. It's basically a delicious game of "telephone", with the final outcome barely resembling the original source!

While I've always considered this to be a Christmas cookie in its earlier incarnations, it's actually a great all-season cookie.

Makes about 24 cookies

Amaretto	1/4 cup	50 ml
Dried cherries	3/4 cup	175 ml
Butter, softened	1/2 cup	125 ml
Granulated sugar	1/2 cup	125 ml
Brown sugar, packed	1/4 cup	50 ml
Large eggs	2	2
Vanilla	1 tsp	5 ml
Brown rice flour	3/4 cup	175 ml
Sorghum flour	1/2 cup	125 ml
Coconut flour	1/4 cup	50 ml
Tapioca starch	1 Tbsp	15 ml
Xanthan gum	1 tsp	5 ml
Baking powder	1/2 tsp	2 ml
Baking soda	1/4 tsp	1 ml
Salt	1/2 tsp	2 ml
Dark chocolate chips	1 cup	250 ml
Shredded coconut	3/4 cup	175 ml

Soak cherries in Amaretto overnight, or - for a non alcoholic version - simmer cherries in Amaretto until soft.

Cream together butter and sugars until fluffy. Add in egg, mix until well incorporated. In a separate bowl, combine flours, tapioca starch, xanthan gum, baking powder, baking soda, and salt. Add to wet mixture, stir until fully incorporated and relatively smooth. Stir in chocolate chips, coconut, and soaked cherries. Chill for 1 hour.

Preheat oven to 350F (180 C). Line 2 baking sheets with parchment paper.

Use a teaspoon to drop very generous – about 1 tbsp – mounds onto cookie sheets. Bake for 12-15 minutes, or until starting to turn a light golden brown on top. (The edges will turn golden earlier than the top.)

Noelles

Strawberry Macarons

French Macarons - The Easy Way

For anyone who's ever looked online to figure out how to make your own macarons, it can be a scary thing. Start working on the cookies 3+ days before you want to serve them. Leave egg whites out on the kitchen table for 3 days to "age" (Um.. Gross). Grind your own nuts. Weigh each ingredient carefully. Sift everything multiple times. Make sure the temperature and humidity outside falls within a very specific range. Baby the meringue. Babysit the cookies. Follow a huge list of instructions and "rules", or expect certain failure.

Oh, and if your cookies are cracked, lack "feet", aren't perfectly round, perfectly smooth, or perfectly... perfect? Well then you just fail as a wife, mother, friend, hostess, and human being. The macaron god obviously hates you.*

At a retail price of $1.50+ per cookie though... ouch. Kinda leaves you stuck between a rock and a macaron-less hard place, huh?

So, I'm pleased to say that I've developed an easy, fool proof way to make perfect macarons. Obscenely delicious macarons! Oh, and I can sum the whole technique up in one word!

RUSTIC.

People, these are cookies, not rocket surgery. COOKIES! They are made to be snarfed, not shellacked and displayed in a museum. If your friends or guests judge you on a lack of a teeny "ruffle"/foot around you cookies, a slightly oblong shape, or having texture (*gasp*!)... let them clutch their pearls elsewhere.

Baking cookies is about doing something you enjoy, and making something tasty and delicious for the ones you love. It should never be about super precision, completing a lengthy set of bizarre rituals, and dying a little every time that someone pops that amount of work into their mouths. So let's drop the fussy nonsense, and stop the macaron insanity! My macarons may be ugly, but they taste a million times better than any I've bought in a store. Besides, ugly is the new cute, right?

Here's the thing. The store bought macarons I've bought have been a little "blah" when it comes to flavour. The meringue cookie part is usually not flavoured at all, and the bakeries seem to go pretty conservative on adding flavours to the filling. Granted, this is Minnesota, so it may be COMPLETELY different elsewhere.

Nonetheless, I like my baked goods to be SO rich and full of flavour, that 1 or 2 is enough to thoroughly satisfy and satiate any sweet cravings for a while. I DO come from the land of the Nanaimo Bar, though... so this may be a cultural thing for me :)

This recipe will take less than 20 minutes from "Hrm. I think I'll make some macarons", to putting those suckers in the oven... and that's being generous (About 10 minutes, for me!). The filling takes about 5 minutes of active work, and actually filling the cookies is probably another 5-10.

Read the instructions first. Take a breath. Get past all of the guilt and shame and pressure that you may have read on other macaron recipes. The fact of the matter is that even seasoned professionals still screw up macarons from time to time, even while following the "rules" religiously. This may or may not give you a "foot", and they may have slightly more texture from the nuts than you're "supposed" to have… but they have that perfect crispy/chewy texture that macaroons are known for… without a hit to your sanity.

Repeat after me: They are just cookies. They. Are. Just. Cookies. Good? Good. Let's do this!

Makes 20-24 cookies

Icing (powdered) sugar	1 1/2 cup	300 ml
Finely ground nuts **	1 cup	250 ml
Large egg whites	3	3
Granulated sugar	4 Tbsp	60 ml
Vanilla extract	1+ tsp	5+ ml
Gel food colouring, if desired		

Preheat your oven to 300 F (150 C). Line baking sheets with parchment paper.

Mix together powdered sugar and ground nuts, set aside.

Mix egg whites and sugar in a *very clean* metal mixer bowl. It is very important that not only is the bowl and whisk attachment VERY clean, but that no specks of egg yolk are included with the egg white. The presence of any egg yolk or grease on your bowl or whisk will prevent the egg whites from properly whipping up. This is the only "rule" you really need to be concerned about!

Affix your bowl to the mixer, and whip eggs on high until stiff peaks form. The whites will be pillowy, thick, and marshmallowy. When you remove the whisk from the meringue, it should leave a very definite "peak" – if the tip flips over a little, that's ok. Add extract and a small amount food colouring -if desired - whisk in.

Dump bowl of dry ingredients into the meringue. Use a wooden spoon or spatula to gently stir the mixture until everything is well incorporated and very thick.

Once mixture is fairly uniform, beat it until it's still thick, but oozes a bit. You don't want to beat it till it's fully RUNNY, but you'd like it to settle back into place if you remove some and drop it back into the mix. It's better to under-beat it than to over-beat it.

Spoon macaron batter into a pastry / frosting bag with a 1/4" or so opening – whether a metal tip, or just the end cut off the bag.

Pipe ~ 1.25" – 1.5" rounds onto prepared baking sheets. If the batter isn't running all, there's no real worry about placing them close together – I'll leave an inch or so between the rounds.

Pick up the sheet of piped cookies, and rap it against the counter a couple of times to dislodge any air bubbles.

Bake cookies for 13-16 minutes, or until they lift easily from the parchment. (Undercooked macarons will stick). Remove from oven, cool to room temperature, and prepare the filling.

Basic White Chocolate Filling

Heavy cream	1/3 cup	75 ml
White chocolate chips	5 oz	140 g

In a small saucepan, heat heavy cream over medium, stirring just until it comes to a boil.

Remove saucepan from heat, add white chocolate chips. Stir mixture until chocolate chips are melted and completely incorporated into the mix, which should be smooth. Allow to cool for about 15 minutes, or until thick enough to fill cookies with.

To assemble Macarons

Spoon or pipe about a tablespoon worth of filling onto the flat underside of one cookie. Top with the underside of another cookie. (Rounded sides facing out).

If any cookies collapsed or get smashed in the course of handling them, spoon the filling into the smashed cavity, leaving the flat side on the outside. Again… it's a cookie.

Done. Snarf em happily!

* I swear, I've seen multiple laments about a temperamental God of Macarons. I can't make this up.

** Finely ground nuts may be referred to as "meal" or "flour", depending on where you find them. It's a specialty item, so it can be difficult to find in stores - I usually order online. You can use whatever kind of nut you like - I'll usually use either pistachios or almonds (almonds being the standard!). Feel free to get fancy with it, and match your favourite nut flavour to the filling. Walnut meal with a pumpkin spice filling, perhaps?

Variations:

Extracts: Substitute your favourite flavour extract in place of the vanilla. Add more, to taste, if you like.

Nut Filling: Make basic white chocolate filling. Use only 1/4 cup of heavy cream, and add 1/4 cup of nut butter of your choice. Whisk together in the first step. I like to use pistachio butter, but there are ALL kinds of nut butters out there!

Caramel Filling: Melt caramels, allow to cool until soft enough to spoon onto cookies. This is especially good when sprinkled with a little sea salt

Fruit Filling: Use your favourite jam or fruit preserves as a filling

Buttercream: Use your favourite buttercream recipe as a filling.

Fruit Macarons: Add 3 Tbsp (45 ml) of fruit powder to the batter, along with the powdered sugar. Look online for fruit powders - They're made from crushing freeze-dried fruit. My favourites for macarons are strawberry and blueberry... and you can even add ~ 2 Tbsp of fruit powder to the white chocolate filling for extra flavour!

Fruitcake Cookies

The fact that this recipe even exists... it's sort of a miracle. You see, I'm one of those people that hate fruitcake. It's not that I buy into mass "ew!" hysteria (I love broccoli and Brussels sprouts, for instance!), it's that I find glaceed / candied fruit to be one of the nastiest things on the planet. I mean, right up there with Velveeta. Gross.

WOW. These are amazing! The substitution of dried fruits for glaceed, the Southern Comfort... it just created this vivid palette of flavour. We used a mix of raisins, cranberries, cherries, apricots, and pineapple, but you can use a combination of whatever dried fruit you love. Oh, and don't worry about buying too much – you'll probably want to put on another batch once you try these.

Makes about 20-24 LARGE cookies

Mixed dried fruit	1 lb	500 g
Southern Comfort *	1 cup	250 ml
Butter, softened	1/4 cup	50 ml
Dark brown sugar, packed	1/4 cup	50 ml
Large eggs	2	2
Finely grated zest of 1 lemon		
Finely grated zest of 1 orange		
Sorghum flour	1/2 cup	125 ml
White rice flour	1/4 cup	50 ml
Coconut flour	1/4 cup	50 ml
Xanthan gum	1 tsp	5 ml
Baking soda	1/2 tsp	2 ml
Ground cinnamon	1 tsp	5 ml
Pecans, chopped	1/2 lb	250 g

A day or two before baking the cookies, chop dried fruits into pieces, mix in Southern Comfort, and cover.

Preheat oven to 325 F (165 C). Line baking sheets with parchment paper, or coat well with baking spray. Strain dried fruit mixture, leaving it in your sieve to drain while you prepare the rest of the cookie batter.

Cream butter and sugar until light and fluffy. Add eggs and zests, continue beating until eggs are fully incorporated and mixture is once again smooth and fluffy. In a separate bowl, combine flours, xanthan gum, baking soda, and cinnamon. Add most of it (reserve about 1/4 cup) to the butter & sugar mixture, beat gently until well combined. Add strained fruit to the reserved flour mixture, toss well to coat the pieces (to separate them a bit). Add coated fruit and pecans to the cookie batter, mix well.

Use a tablespoon, cookie scoop, or small ice cream scoop to drop rounded spoonfuls of the batter onto prepared baking sheets. Bake for 15-20 minutes, until golden brown. Allow to cool on sheets for 5 minutes or so, before gently transferring to baking racks to finish cooling. Once cookies are cool, keep them stored in airtight containers. Much like actual fruitcake, these tend to get even better with age!

* Southern Comfort is my favourite spirit to use in making fruitcake, but be aware: Southern Comfort is made from Bourbon, a spirit that is often distilled from (among other things) fermented wheat. While it doesn't cause a reaction in MOST people with gluten sensitivities - and the leading Celiac associations have deemed it gluten-free as of publication of this book - a few experts disagree. If you have noticed a reaction, or just want to play it extra safe, it could be a good idea forgo the Southern Comfort in favour of rum or brandy.

If you're looking to do an alcohol free version, simmer the dried fruit in juice or non-alcoholic wine it just until the fruit softens up and soaks up most of the liquid.

Fruitcake

Forget everything you've heard about fruitcake! This is a gorgeous, extremely tasty fruitcake that will be loved by all – fans of regular fruitcake, fruitcake haters, people with gluten allergies, and even those who aren't restricted to gluten free.

This cake? I'd eat this for breakfast, in addition to as a snack, or dessert. I'll be making variations of this throughout the year, to satisfy any urge for baked goods. This is WAY too good to be designated JUST a holiday thing! We used a mix of raisins, cranberries, cherries, apricots, and pineapple, but you can use a combination of whatever dried fruit you love. Apples, blackberries, cantaloupe – so much variety out there! Just go for the more natural, chewy type dried fruit. Banana chips, freeze dried, etc won't work as well.

Mixed dried fruit	1 lb	500 g
Southern Comfort *	2/3 cup	150 ml
Butter, softened	1/2 cup	125 ml
Granulated sugar	3/4 cup	175 ml
Large eggs, separated	3	3
Vanilla extract	1 tsp	5 ml
Finely grated zest of 1 lemon		
Finely grated zest of 1 orange		
Sorghum flour	1/2 cup	125 ml
White rice flour	1/4 cup	50 ml
Coconut flour	1/4 cup	50 ml
Xanthan gum	1 tsp	5 ml
Baking powder	1 1/2 tsp	7 ml
Salt	1/2 tsp	2 ml
Milk	1/2 cup	125 ml
Chopped pecans	1 cup	250 ml

A day or two before baking the fruitcake, chop dried fruits into pieces, mix in Southern Comfort, and cover.

When ready to make the fruitcake, Preheat oven to 325 F (165 C). Spray an 8" round cake pan (spring form pan works, also), and then line it with parchment paper. I like to cut a round just slightly bigger than the bottom diameter of the pan, centering it, and smoothing the edges slightly up the side of the pan, folding and easing as necessary. Then, I cut a "collar" of parchment, about 5" x 28". Fold that in half along the length, and then place that – folded side down – around the inside edge of the cake pan.

Strain dried fruit mixture, leaving it in your sieve to drain while you prepare the rest of the cookie batter. Be sure to reserve the Southern Comfort / fruit syrup that strains out!

Cream butter and sugar until light and fluffy. Add egg YOLKS (reserving the whites separately), vanilla, and zests, continue beating until eggs are fully incorporated and mixture is once again smooth and fluffy.

In a separate bowl, combine flours, xanthan gum, baking powder, and salt. Add dry ingredients to the butter & sugar mixture, beat gently until well combined. Add milk, continuing to beat until well combined. Add in the strained fruits, mixing once more until well combined. Set aside.

In a – very clean – mixing bowl or stand mixer, whip the egg whites on high speed, until stiff peaks form. Gently fold whipped egg whites into the main batter, until all of the "white" disappears. Gently mix in the pecans, just until well distributed.

Pour cake batter into prepared cake pan, smooth around the pan to push the parchment paper "collar" against the sides of the pan. Gently bang the pan onto a flat surface a few times to knock out any air bubbles.

Bake for about an hour and a half – hour and 45 minutes, until a knife poked into the center of the cake comes out clean.

While cake is still hot, pour reserved Southern Comfort runoff evening over the top of the cake. Allow to cool fully before removing from pan.

* Southern Comfort is my favourite spirit to use in making fruitcake, but be aware: Southern Comfort is made from Bourbon, is a spirit that is often distilled from (among otehr things) fermented wheat. While it doesn't cause a reaction in MOST people with gluten sensitivities - and the leading Celiac associations have deemed it gluten-free as of publication of this book - a few experts disagree. If you have noticed a reaction, or just want to play it extra safe, it could be a good idea forgo the Southern Comfort in favour of rum or brandy.

Fruitcake

193

Butter Tarts

Butter tarts are another delicacy from my homeland. They've been around forever, and you can get them anywhere in Canada… bakeries.. gas stations.. even boxes of factory made ones. Because they've been around forever, there are about a million versions of it. Some use brown sugar, some use white… most use corn syrup, I use maple… you get the idea.

(Makes about 18-20 butter tarts)

White rice flour	3/4 cup	175 ml
Light buckwheat flour	3/4 cup	175 ml
Millet flour	1/2 cup	125 ml
Sweet rice flour	1/4 cup	50 ml
Corn starch, plus extra for rolling	1/4 cup	50 ml
Granulated sugar	2 Tbsp	30 ml
Xanthan gum	2 tsp	10 ml
Cream cheese	8 oz	250 g
Cold butter	1/2 cup	125 ml
Large egg	1	1
Cold water	1/4 cup	50 ml
Raisins	1/2 – 1 cup	125-250 ml
Butter, softened	1/3 cup	75 ml
Light brown sugar, packed	1 cup	250 ml
Pure maple syrup	1/4 cup	50 ml
Large eggs, whisked*	2	2

Measure flours, corn starch, sugar and xanthan gum into the bowl of your food processor, blitz to combine. Add cream cheese, butter, and egg, blitz a few times until mixture resembles gravel. Stream in cold water as you run the food processor, just long enough to bring it together as a dough.

Remove dough from processor, knead lightly to bring it together as a ball. Wrap in plastic film, chill for 1 hour.

Lightly dust your work surface with extra corn starch, roll chilled dough out pretty thin – 1/8" to 1/4", depending on your tastes – some prefer a thinner shell, some thicker. Cut 4" rounds from the pastry.

Carefully transfer the pastry rounds to a lightly greased muffin pan. I like to flatten the bottom against the tin, and work out from there, flattening the whole round to be flush with the muffin pan cavity – it holds the most filling! Feel free to get decorative about it – flattening the bottom of the dough against the muffin pan, gently ruffling the edges… it's up to you! Chill the pan of prepared tart shells until ready to use.

Preheat oven to 375 F (190 C)

Divide raisins among tart shells – I personally like to have a fair amount of raisins in my butter tarts, so I use 1-2 cups. (1/2 cup is probably closer to average!). Set aside.

Combine butter, brown sugar, and maple syrup in a medium saucepan. Beat until smooth. Add in eggs, beat once more until well combined. Heat mixture on medium, stirring constantly. Bring mixture JUST to a boil, remove from heat. Carefully pour mixture into prepared tart shells.

Bake for 15-20 minutes, until filling has set and the pastry is lightly browned. Remove from oven and allow to cool. These are usually served at room temperature, but some prefer them chilled!

* I like my butter tarts slightly runny. Add an extra egg for a firmer filling.

Butter Tarts

Mousse

When it comes to mousse, there are two main styles - "Traditional" and "Easy". Traditional mousse is made with raw egg yolks and/or egg whites. While this is perfectly safe for the vast majority of the population, pregnant women, the elderly, and immune compromised individuals may want to opt for the Easy version, which does not contain any raw eggs.

Basic Mousse (Easy)

Unflavoured gelatin powder	1 1/2 tsp	7 ml
Cold water	1/3 cup	75 ml
Granulated sugar	1/3 cup	75 ml
Heavy cream	2 cups	500 ml
Vanilla Extract	1 tsp	5 ml

In a small bowl, sprinkle gelatin over water and allow to soak for 5 minutes. Transfer bowl to microwave, heat in 10 second increments until gelatin dissolves into the water.

Combine sugar and heavy cream together in a mixing bowl. Whip until stiff peaks form, then carefully fold in the vanilla and gelatin mixture, stirring until combined. Pour into 6-8 serving glasses, chill until set, about 2 hours.

Basic Chocolate Mousse (Easy)

Chocolate of choice	12 oz	340 g
Butter	4 Tbsp	60 ml
Heavy cream	1 3/4 cups	425 ml
Unflavoured gelatin powder	1 tsp	5 ml
Cold water	1/3 cup	75 ml
Vanilla extract	1 tsp	5 ml

Combine chocolate, butter, and heavy cream in the top of a double boiler. Melt together over simmering water, stirring until smooth. Cool to room temperature, then chill until cold.

In a small bowl, sprinkle gelatin over water and allow to soak for 5 minutes. Transfer bowl to microwave, heat in 10 second increments until gelatin dissolves into the water.

Whip chilled chocolate mixture until stiff peaks form, then carefully fold in the vanilla and gelatin mixture, stirring until combined. Pour into 6-8 serving glasses, chill until set, about 2 hours.

Basic Mousse (Traditional)

Granulated sugar	1/4 cup	50 ml
Egg yolks	2	2
Heavy cream	1 cup	250 ml
Egg whites	3	3
Vanilla extract	1 tsp	5 ml

Combine sugar and egg yolks together, beat until pale yellow and fluffy. Stir in heavy cream a little at a time, until fully incorporated. Whip until stiff peaks form, transfer to fridge.

In a separate bowl, whip the egg whites until stiff peaks form. Carefully fold in chilled whipped cream mixture along with vanilla, stirring until combined. Pour into 4-6 serving glasses, chill until set, about 2 hours.

Basic Fruit Mousse

Fruit puree *	1 cup	250 ml
Granulated sugar	1/4 cup	50 ml
Unflavoured gelatin powder	3 tsp	15 ml
Cold Water	1/3 cup	75 ml
Large egg whites	2	2
Heavy cream	1 cup	250 ml
Vanilla extract	1 tsp	5 ml

Combine fruit puree and sugar together in a large bowl, set aside.

In a small bowl, sprinkle gelatin over water and allow to soak for 5 minutes. Transfer bowl to microwave, heat in 10 second increments until gelatin dissolves into the water. Pour into fruit puree mixture, stir until well incorporated, then chill while preparing the rest of the ingredients.

In a separate bowl, whip egg whites until stiff peaks form. Carefully fold into chilled fruit mixture, stirring until combined.

Whip cream and vanilla until stiff peaks form, then carefully fold in to the fruit mixture, stirring until combined. Pour into 6-8 serving glasses, chill until set, about 2 hours.

* If you have access to pre made fruit puree, that is easiest. Certain fruits - such as berries - puree well without any cooking. More firm fruits, such as pears, should be chopped and cooked until soft before pureeing. If you want to be really quick and dirty about it, you can puree canned fruit - strain the liquid off first!

Certain fruits - such as pineapple, papaya, and kiwi fruit - contain enzymes that break down the protein strands in gelatin. It is important to thoroughly cook these fruits before using them in this recipe. Another alternative would be to use canned, as they are pre-cooked.

Fresh Raspberry Mousse

Basic Chocolate Mousse (Traditional)

Chocolate of choice	4 ½ oz	140 g
Butter	2 Tbsp	30 ml
Heavy cream	1 cup	250 ml
Large eggs, separated	3	3
Granulated sugar	1 Tbsp	15 ml
Vanilla extract	1 tsp	5 ml

Combine chocolate, butter, and heavy cream in the top of a double boiler. Melt together over simmering water, stirring until smooth. Cool to almost room temperature.

Combine egg yolks, sugar, and vanilla together, beat until pale yellow and fluffy. Stir in chocolate mixture a little at a time, until fully incorporated. Transfer to fridge, chill completely.

Whip chilled chocolate mixture until stiff peaks form. In a separate bowl, whip the egg whites until stiff peaks form. Carefully fold in chilled chocolate mixture, stirring until combined. Pour into 4-6 serving glasses, chill until set, about 2 hours.

Doughnut Holes

Doughnut Holes

As a Canadian living in the USA, I've had to endure powerful cravings for Tim Horton's "Timbits" every once in a while... and discovering my gluten issues didn't do anything to stop those cravings.

I came up with a quick gluten-free version back in 2012, utilizing commercially available all-purpose gluten-free flour. They were pretty ok - good, even - but were definitely not the real deal.

After much in the way of tweaking the recipe, I'm proud to present this gluten-free version. It's great in its most basic form - vanilla, unglazed doughnuts - but half the point of doughnut holes is variety. With just a few extra bowls and a small amount of effort, you can turn a basic batch of doughnut holes into a feast for the eyes AND stomach!

Makes about 30

Vegetable oil for frying		
Milk	1 1/2 cup	375 ml
Lemon juice	1/4 cup	50 ml
Large egg	1	1
Vegetable oil	2 tsp	10 ml
Vanilla extract	1-2 tsp	5-10 ml
Sorghum flour	1 cup	250 ml
White rice flour	2/3 cup	150 ml
Potato starch	1/3 cup	75 ml
Coconut flour	1/3 cup	75 ml
Tapioca starch	2 Tbsp	30 ml
Granulated sugar	3/4 cup	175 ml
Baking soda	1 1/2 tsp	7 ml
Salt	1 tsp	5 ml
Xanthan gum	1 tsp	5 ml

Heat oil to 375 F (190 C). You can use a deep fryer, or a heavy pan. If not using a deep fryer, use a deep, heavy pot, filled to at least 3" deep.

Whisk together milk, lemon juice, egg, vegetable oil, and vanilla until well combined and smooth, set aside.

In a large mixing bowl, combine remaining (dry) ingredients. Add wet ingredients to dry, stirring with a whisk until well incorporated. Allow to sit for 10 minutes.

Using two teaspoons, scoop out approximately 1" balls of dough, carefully dropping them into the hot oil. (Do NOT splash yourself!).* Cook for about 3 minutes, flip doughnut holes onto their other sides, cook for another 2-3 minutes. Cook a few donuts at a time, being careful to not over crowd your fryer / pot.

When doughnut holes are cooked, use a (metal!) slotted spoon to transfer them from the oil, to a pan lined with paper towels. Once all donuts are cooked, allow to cool for a few minutes.

* Dropping the doughnut holes as described is the quickest, cleanest version - but the resulting doughnut holes will be irregular. To get nicely smooth, round doughnut holes, carefully roll the blobs of dough between moistened hands before gently adding to the hot oil.

Vanilla Doughnut Glaze

Water	1/2 cup	125 ml
Vanilla	1/2 tsp	2 ml
Salt	pinch	pinch
Icing (powdered) sugar	3+ cups	750+ ml

Whisk together water, vanilla, and salt. Add powdered sugar, a cup or so at a time, whisking until thick (but still "dip-able") and completely smooth. Transfer to a coffee mug or other narrow/tall vessel. Use a couple of forks to dip each)completely cooled!) donut hole – one at a time – turning to coat completely. Allow excess glaze to drip off doughnut before placing on parchment paper to dry.

Chocolate Doughnut Glaze

Water	1/2 cup	125 ml
Vanilla	1/2 tsp	2 ml
Salt	pinch	pinch
Cocoa powder	1/3 cup	75 ml
Icing (powdered) sugar	2+ cups	500+ ml

Whisk together water, vanilla, and salt. Add cocoa powder, whisking until smooth. Add powdered sugar, a cup or so at a time, whisking until thick (but still "dip-able") and completely smooth. Transfer to a coffee mug or other narrow/tall vessel. Use a couple of forks to dip each (completely cooled!) donut hole – one at a time – turning to coat completely. Allow excess glaze to drip off doughnut before placing on parchment paper to dry.

Honey Dip

Liquid honey	2/3 cup	150 ml
Water	1/4 cup	50 ml

In a medium saucepan, whisk together honey and water until honey is fully dissolved in water. Bring to a boil, turn heat down, and simmer for 3 minutes. Remove from heat, allow to cool completely before dipping cooled doughnut holes.

Other Variations:

Sugar coated: Roll hot doughnut holes in granulated sugar... or roll cooled doughnut holes in powdered sugar.

Dutchie: Add 3/4 cup (175 ml) raisins to batter. Allow fried doughnuts to cool completely before dipping in vanilla doughnut glaze

Chocolate glazed: Add 1/4 cup (50 ml) cocoa in place of 1/4 cup of the sorghum flour in the batter. Allow fried doughnuts to cool completely before dipping in vanilla or chocolate doughnut glaze

Cinnamon sugar: After rolling hot doughnut holes on paper towels - but before allowing them to cool - roll in doughnut holes in cinnamon sugar : 1/2 cup (125 ml) sugar to 2 Tbsp (30 ml) cinnamon, or to taste.

Apple fritter: Add 1 tsp (5 ml) cinnamon and a pinch of cloves to the dry ingredients. Peel and chop (about 1/4" pieces for doughnut holes, 1/2" for larger fritters) 1 small apple, add to batter after wet and dry ingredients have been mixed together.

Filled/sugared: Fit a pastry bag with a fairly wide (1/4"-1/2") metal piping tip. Fill bag with jam, pudding, or pie filling of choice. Jab metal tip into the side of a fully cooled doughnut hole, squeeze a small amount of filling into the doughnut. Roll in powdered sugar to finish.

Chai: Add 2 Tbsp (30 ml) instant black tea, 1/2 tsp (2 ml) each of cinnamon and cardamom, and 1/4 tsp (1 ml) each nutmeg, and ground cloves to the dry ingredients in the batter

Coconut: Dip in glaze, roll in coconut (toasted or regular)

Cream Puffs and more

Cream puffs, eclairs, and profiteroles are great "fancy" dessert options. Not only are they impressive, they are easier to make than you may expect, they take very little in the way of ingredients, and can be customized many ways.

Each of these desserts start out with the batter - Pâte à choux, or "choux pastry". It's a basic recipe that's used to make everything from cream puffs and eclairs to crullers and churros. It doesn't contain any leavening ingredients (yeast, baking powder, baking soda, etc), instead relying on its high moisture content to puff during baking. Baked at a high temperature, the water becomes steam and creates large air pockets in the final product. Fill them however you want – with pastry cream, pudding, mousse – and there you go. Fancy dessert!

Milk	1 cup	250 ml
Butter	1/2 cup	125 ml
Granulated sugar	1 tsp	5 ml
Salt	1/2 tsp	2 ml
Sweet rice flour	1/3 cup	75 ml
White rice flour	1/3 cup	75 ml
Millet flour	1/3 cup	75 ml
Xanthan	1 tsp	5 ml
Baking powder	1/2 tsp	2 ml
Large eggs	3	3
Large egg whites	2	2

Preheat oven to 400 F (200 C) . Line a baking sheet with parchment paper or a nonstick baking sheet. It's very important to not grease the pan - it will cause the pastries to flatten!

Combine milk, butter, sugar, and salt in a medium sauce pan, heat to a boil. In a separate bowl, combine flours, xanthan gum, and baking powder. Remove from heat, add flour mixture, stirring until well incorporated. Reduce heat to medium, return saucepan to stove top. Cook for another minute or so, until the dough comes together, leaving the sides of the pan. Transfer dough to the bowl of your mixer. Using the paddle attachment, beat the dough for a minute or so to allow it to cool slightly.

Meanwhile, beat together eggs and egg whites in a small bowl. With the mixer set to medium, add egg mixture to dough a little at a time, allowing eggs to fully incorporate into the dough before adding more. It may look like a separating mess, but I promise it will come together!

When all of the eggs are incorporated and the dough is smooth and shiny, it's ready to pipe! It'll be soft and a bit sticky, but more or less be able to hold its shape. Pipe it out according to your desired use (below), and bake for the time indicated.

Cream Puffs:
Using a pastry bag with a medium/ large round or star tip, pipe out rounds that are about 2-2.5" in diameter and 1 ½" tall, leaving 2-3" between mounds.. Use a moistened finger to pat down any peaks of dough that may form as you finish piping each.

Bake for 12 minutes, then -WITHOUT opening the oven door - turn the temperature down to 350 F (180 C) and bake for another 35 minutes. Crack the oven door open a few inches, turn the heat off, and allow the puffs to cool in the oven for 30 minutes. This step allows the insides to dry out, providing a stronger structure to prevent collapse.

Once puffs are completely cool, cut in half horizontally, and fill with your choice of pastry cream, pudding, whipped cream, or mousse. Dust with powdered sugar, drizzle with chocolate, and/or serve with fresh fruit or berries!

Profiteroles:
Using spoons or a pastry bags, make tablespoon-sized mounds of batter, leaving 2" of space between each. Use a moistened finger to pat down any peaks of dough that may form as you finish piping each.

Bake for 12 minutes, then -WITHOUT opening the oven door - turn the temperature down to 350 F (180 C) and bake for another 25 minutes. Crack the oven door open a few inches, turn the heat off, and allow the puffs to cool in the oven for 30 minutes. This step allows the insides to dry out, providing a stronger structure to prevent collapse.

Fill a pastry bag with your choice of pastry cream, pudding, or mousse. Once puffs are completely cool, jam the tip of the pastry bag into the side of a puff, and fill! Dust with powdered sugar, drizzle with chocolate, and/or serve with fresh fruit or berries. Can also be used to make croquembouche.

Eclairs:
Using a pastry bag with a large round or star tip, pipe out logs that are about 2" x 5-6" leaving 2" between logs. Use a moistened finger to pat down any peaks of dough that may form as you finish piping each.

Bake for 12 minutes, then -WITHOUT opening the oven door - turn the temperature down to 350 F (180 C) and bake for another 30 minutes. Crack the oven door open a few inches, turn the heat off, and allow the puffs to cool in the oven for 30 minutes. This step allows the insides to dry out, providing a stronger structure to prevent collapse.

Once logs are completely cool, cut in half horizontally, and fill with your choice of pastry cream, pudding, or mousse. Dip the tops in chocolate glaze, chill.

Mini Eclairs:
Using a pastry bag with a medium/ large round or star tip, pipe out logs that are about 1" x 2" leaving 2" between logs. Use a moistened finger to pat down any peaks of dough that may form as you finish piping each.

Bake for 12 minutes, then -WITHOUT opening the oven door - turn the temperature down to 350 F (180 C) and bake for another 20 minutes. Crack the oven door open a few inches, turn the heat off, and allow the puffs to cool in the oven for 30 minutes. This step allows the insides to dry out, providing a stronger structure to prevent collapse.

Fill a pastry bag with your choice of pastry cream, pudding, or mousse. Once puffs are completely cool, jam the tip of the pastry bag into the side of a puff, and fill! Dip the tops in chocolate glaze (recipe below), chill.

Chocolate Glaze

Semi sweet chocolate	4 oz	125 g
Heavy cream	½ cup	125 ml

Finely chop chocolate, place into a glass mixing bowl, and put aside.

In a small saucepan, heat heavy cream to a boil, remove from heat. Pour hot cream into the bowl of chocolate. Let sit for 3-5 minutes. Starting in the middle of the bowl, slowly start stirring the chocolate and cream until all of the chocolate is melted and the cream has disappeared into it – it should be smooth.

Glaze can be made a day or two in advance and kept - covered - in the refrigerator. Warm in the microwave for 20-30 seconds when ready to use.

Cream Puffs

Individual Chocolate Croquembouche

1 batch profiteroles, chilled		
Chocolate of choice	10 oz	275 g

Finely chop the chocolate (if not using chocolate chips), place in a microwave safe glass dish. Microwave on high for 20 seconds at a time until about half melted. Stir until completely melted.

Divide profiteroles between number of servings needed. Ideally, you'll want 8, but that will vary greatly based on how large you made them! Assuming 8 small puffs, assemble them like this:

Dip the bottom of a cream puff in chocolate, place on small serving plate. Repeat with 3 more puffs, forming a square. You'll be using the melted chocolate to "glue" the profiteroles to the plate - and to each other as you go. Dip the bottoms of 3 more puffs into chocolate, arranging on top of the first 4 puffs. Top with 1 more dipped profiterole, to form a pyramid shape. Repeat with remaining servings, chill until chocolate sets up hard - at least 30 minutes.

To serve, drizzle with more chocolate, dust with powdered sugar, or pipe on some whipped cream. This is best served the same day - otherwise, the puffs can get soggy.

Pastry Cream

Homemade pastry cream is one of my favourite fillings for anything made with pâte à choux. Not only does it taste better than store bought versions (including, say, instant pudding), I think it's fun to do the start-to-finish thing… and gives you huge bragging rights. Also, it's not difficult at all, or even all THAT time consuming. The pastry cream can be made ahead and chilled until use.

Large egg yolks	3	3
Granulated sugar	1/4 cup	50 ml
Cornstarch	1 Tbsp	15 ml
Half and half	1 cup	250 ml
Butter	2 Tbsp	30 ml
Vanilla extract, to taste	1-2 tsp	5-10 ml

Whisk yolks together with sugar until fluffy and pale yellow. Add Cornstarch, whisk until incorporated and smooth. Set aside.

In a small saucepan, bring liqueur and milk to a light boil. Measure about 1/4 cup (50 ml) of the hot milk liquid, and stream slowly into egg mixture while whisking. Continue streaming liquid and whisking until it is completely incorporated, and mixture is smooth. Repeat with another 1/4 cup (50 ml) of hot liquid.

Remove saucepan from heat, pour egg mixture into milk mixture, whisking constantly. Once fully incorporated and smooth, return to heat. Turn heat down to low. Continue whisking mixture constantly, cooking until mixture is very thick. Remove from heat, whisk in butter and vanilla extract until fully incorporated and smooth. Cover with plastic wrap, chill until needed.

* For a more adult option, substitute 1/2 cup of cream liqueur of your choice for 1/2 cup of the Half and half. Don't have Half and half? Use 1/2 cup milk and 1/2 cup heavy cream!

Pavlova

Pavlovas are my absolute favorite dessert of all time! They're basically a type of large meringue - one which is crispy on the outside, and like a giant, fluffy marshmallow on the inside! - heaped with whipped cream, then topped with fruit. Does it get any better? No. No, it doesn't! I love exposing people to this dessert, I love watching their eyes pop when they bite in to a pav for the first time. Also: they're inherently gluten-free!

Pavlovas are either an Australian dessert, or a New Zealand dessert, depending on who you ask. The two of them have a lot of national pride wrapped up in Pavlova wars, and in my mind, if there's something worth fighting over, it's Pavlova. Legend has it that a chef in one of the two countries was so enamored with Anna Pavlova - a famous ballerina in the early 20th century - that he created this dessert in her honor. Can you imagine having a man so in love with you, that he'd create perfection itself? Amazing. I digress. The fluffy meringue base and whipped cream are said to represent her tutus.

Nice light texture, and a wonderful way to enjoy fresh fruit. Perfect summer dessert for entertaining, and this is a really easy recipe for anyone. A quick head's up though - if your meringue is not cracked by the time you remove it from the oven, it will likely crack at some other point, and will almost certainly crack when you start garnishing. Don't worry! Totally normal, no one will notice or care!

As with most/all recipes that require egg whites for structure, it is brutally important that the egg whites are completely free of ANY egg yolk bits. I'm not kidding - not even a speck. Even a tiny amount will prevent them from whipping up like they're supposed to. If you're not very confident in your egg-cracking prowess, try cracking them individually into a little bowl before transferring them to the mixer. If you get a bit of egg yolk in one, you can just chuck it without ruining the whole batch. Also, be sure that your mixer and whisk attachment are very clean, free from any grease at all. Serves 4-6. (Or 2 Pavlova fanatics! Or one, if it's ME! Muaha!)

Large egg whites	4	4
Super fine / castor sugar*	1 cup	250 ml
Salt	1/8 tsp	1/2 ml
Vanilla extract	2 tsp	10 ml
White vinegar	2 tsp	10 ml
Cornstarch	1 tsp	5 ml
Heavy cream	1 1/4 cup	300 ml
Vanilla extract	1 tsp	5 ml
Granulated sugar, optional	2 Tbsp	30 ml
Fresh Fruits & Berries		

Preheat oven to 350 F (180 C). Remove eggs from fridge and allow to warm to room temp (about 5 minutes). Line a baking sheet with parchment paper, and set aside. Fit your electric mixer with the whisk attachment. In your mixer bowl, beat egg whites together with salt until glossy peaks form. Slowly add in the sugar, and continue whipping until stiff peaks form. Turn off mixer, remove bowl. Sprinkle extract, vinegar, and cornstarch over meringue, gently fold in till combined.

Heap meringue onto the center of your baking sheet. Use a spatula to spread the meringue out to approximately an 8-9" circle. I like to have my meringue a fairly even depth throughout - some like a mound, some like it to be a little concave. If you want to get really fancy, put the meringue into a pastry bag and pipe it out as a mass of swirls that form your 8" circle! It's really up to you!

Put the baking sheet into your oven, and immediately turn the temperature down to 250 F (120 C). Bake for 1 hour and 20 minutes. Once your timer goes off, turn the oven off and let the meringue cool in the oven for several hours. The baking of the meringue can be done the day before, if needed.

Just before serving, whip the heavy cream, together with vanilla and sugar, if using.. I like my Pavlovas a little sweeter, so I add about 2 Tbsp of sugar - add as much or as little as you want. Purists may not want to sweeten the cream at all! Mound the whipped cream on your Pavlova, and top with fresh fruits. Serve immediately!

* Super fine / castor sugar is granulated sugar with a much finer grain size than regular granulated sugar. It is NOT powdered / icing sugar! Super fine sugar is usually sold near the sugar in the baking aisle, in small boxes - sometimes resembling milk cartons. If you aren't able to find actual super fine sugar, you can process regular granulated sugar in your food processor until fine. Measure AFTER you process.

Variations & Ideas

The possibilities for flavouring your Pavlova are endless! Use any non-cream based liqueur to flavour the meringue, or use it as a great venue for displaying your homemade flavour extracts from the first chapter. Use anything you want to flavour the cream, and top with any combination of fruits that strikes your fancy. It really is a truly versatile, amazing dessert. Here are a few of my favorite combinations:

- Rum extract in the both the meringue and whipped cream. Top with sliced bananas, mango, and toasted coconut.

- Rum extract in the both the meringue and whipped cream. Marinate sliced mangos in rum overnight. Top whipped cream with a drizzle of mango puree, marinated mangos, a squeeze of lime juice, and thinly sliced fresh mint leaves.

- Grand Marnier or orange extract in both the meringue and whipped cream. Top with sliced strawberries and kiwis, drizzle with 1 Tbsp grand marnier.

- Almond extract in both the meringue and whipped cream. Top with strawberries, raspberries, and blueberries, garnishing with fresh mint leaves.

- Green tea extract in meringue and whipped cream. Top with thin slices of honeydew and cantaloupe.

- Substitute half of the sugar with light brown sugar. Use rum flavouring in the meringue & whipped cream. Top with cooled bananas foster and pecans!

Pavlova

Wine Poached Pears
210

Poached Fruit

Here's a recipe that's going to take a large amount of space to deal with, when it's actually wickedly simple. Tons of options, that's all!

Poached fruit is a great way to use fruit when it's either off-season and less than perfect, or just a bit under ripe. The fruit is cooked in a flavourful liquid - usually wine - that is sweetened with sugar and/or honey, and flavoured with any number of ingredients.

This cooking process sweetens and softens the fruit, so you're actually quite a bit better off starting with firm and under-ripe! Stone fruit - peaches, nectarines, apricots, plums, etc - are great to work with, but apples and pears (Bosc works best!) are also popular choices. The key is to go with a firm fruit that won't just turn to mush when poached.

Along with the base recipe, you'll find many flavour combinations to try - or just run wild with your own imagination! Poached fruit is great when served as slices on top of cheesecakes (or other desserts), on ice cream... served in halves or as whole fruit. A whole poached pear, perched in a martini glass and drizzled with a little chocolate is a statement kind of dessert!

Let's look at a gorgeous photo of sangria poached pears, before getting to the recipe. Ah, the joys of formatting a cookbook!

Large fruit of choice	4	4
Liquid of choice *	3 cups	750 ml
Granulated sugar	3/4 - 1 cup	175-250 ml
Flavouring items of choice *		

Prepare the fruit. All fruit should be peeled. For most stone fruits, it helps to boil the fruit for a couple of minutes, then run under cold water. This helps loosen the skin, and will enable it to peel off easily. After removing skin, remove pit or core, and halve or slice the fruit thickly, if desired.

In a medium saucepan, combine your liquid(s) of choice with sugar, bring to a boil. Cook, stirring until all sugar is dissolved. Turn the heat down to low, add flavouring items of choice. At this point, it's a good idea to taste the syrup to make sure that the liquid is sweet enough for your taste.

Add the fruit to the pot. If the fruit floats, laying a small, heat proof dish on top of it to weigh it down works well. Cover the pot and allow the fruit to cook through to desired softness - this may happen in 10 minutes, it may take 40-60 minutes. Just poke it every once in awhile to see how it's doing.

Once fruit is cooked through, remove from heat and allow to cool to room temperature. Once cool, move to fridge to chill for at least an hour.

When ready to serve, remove fruit from poaching liquid. To make a sauce to serve with the fruit, return the poaching liquid to the stove top, simmer until reduced in volume and thickened.

* Liquid choices: Wine - red, white, rose, champagne, mead - any type that you like drinking. Favorite spirits, such as rum, whisky, and brandy can also be used. Fruit juice or water can be added for extra flavour, or to cut too-strong flavours.

* Flavouring items of choice: Vanilla beans (cut in half, lengthwise), whole cloves, zest/juice of citrus fruits, tea bags, cinnamon sticks, mint leaves, rosemary... whatever you feel like using! I recommend not using too many different flavours - I like to let the flavour of the fruit shine through.

Flavour Ideas:

- Peaches poached in 1 cup (250 ml) each: Southern Comfort, water, and peach nectar. I like to add about 3/4 cup (175 ml) pecans for the poaching time.

- Pears poached in 1 ½ cups (375 ml) each water and brandy, with a little fresh ginger OR cardamom to taste.

- Apples poached in 1 ½ cups (375 ml) each apple cider and brandy, with a couple whole cloves, 1 vanilla bean, 2 cinnamon sticks, a pinch of nutmeg, and a handful of dried cranberries.

- ANYTHING poached in mead with zests and juice of satsuma oranges and a little squeeze of fresh lemon juice

Pie Crust

Back when I was writing "The Spirited Baker", I managed to obtain some heirloom information from my extended family: great uncle Tom's pie crust recipe, and permission to publish it. You see, I may not be the biggest fan of making pie, but he's renowned for his - they're reportedly scooped out of his hands on sight!

It was his pie recipe that I used as a base for making a gluten-free pie recipe. This makes a flavourful crust with a great texture, that can be used for any of your favourite pie recipes - I'm including a few of my favourites.

Makes 2 pie crust rounds.

Water	1/3 cup	75 ml
Large egg	1	1
Vinegar	1 tsp	5 ml
Sorghum flour	3/4 cup	175 ml
White rice flour	1/2 cup	125 ml
Millet flour	1/2 cup	125 ml
Sweet rice flour	1/4 cup	50 ml
Tapioca starch	1 Tbsp	15 ml
Brown sugar, packed	1 Tbsp	15 ml
Xanthan gum	1 tsp	5 ml
Baking powder	pinch	pinch
Salt	pinch	pinch
Lard or shortening*	1/3 cup	75 ml

Whisk water, egg, and vinegar together, set aside. In a larger bowl, mix together flours, brown sugar, xanthan gum, baking powder, and salt until well combined.

Add wet ingredients to the bowl of dry ingredients, mixing with a fork until just combined. Add lard, cut in with a pastry cutter or fork gently, until it resembles gravel. Don't over handle it. In Tom's words, "Mix it with kindness"!

Gather dough into a loose ball, divide into 6 equal balls. Wrap each with plastic wrap, and let rest for 30 minutes before using.

Bake, following specific pie recipe instructions.

* Tom recommend using Tenderflake brand lard, which is apparently only available in Canada. Shortening can be substituted if lard cannot be obtained, but is definitely not *preferable* to lard.

Partridgeberry Pie

Partridgeberry Pie

Fun trivia: photos of this pie are kind of "Tumblr famous". The day I baked up this pie to shoot for this book, we had another - VERY different - photo shoot with a friend of ours... and this pie was used as a prop. So, if you've seen photos of Thranduil (in a frilly apron), Legolas, and/or Ned the Piemaker in my kitchen... yep, that would be this pie.

Partridgeberries - AKA "lingonberries", regionally - are the key ingredient in my favourite pie recipe. They're something like a cross between a cranberry and a blueberry, and I LOVE them.

Fresh or frozen partridgeberries*	3 cups	750 ml
Granulated sugar	1 1/2 cups	375 ml
Cornstarch	2-3 tsp	10-15 ml
Zest of one orange		
Salt	pinch	pinch
1 batch pie crusts (Page 213)		
Large egg, whisked	1	1
Granulated sugar	2 Tbsp	30 ml

Place berries in a medium saucepan. Whisk together sugar and cornstarch (use 2 tsp for a slightly runnier filling, 3 for a thicker one. We used 3 for the pie pictured!), and add to the berries along with orange zest and salt.

Bring mixture to a boil, stirring frequently. The berries will break down a bit, and the mixture will thicken slightly. Allow to boil for 3 minutes before removing from heat. Allow to cool to room temperature – it will thicken more as it cools.

Preheat oven to 425 F (220 C)

Roll your two crusts out to about 1/4" thick. Line a pie pan with one crust, and cut the other into 1" strips. Transfer cooled filling into the pie shell, spreading to cover the bottom of the pie evenly.

Use the strips of pie crust to create a lattice on top. Where this filling is very dark and stains easily, I don't usually do a properly woven lattice – that involves placing and folding back strips to weave other strips through… and can get pie filling all over the place!

I lay one of the longest strips right across the middle of the pie, vertically. Then I cross it with another of the longest strips, horizontally. The next longest strip gets laid aside the first strip laid, then the next one beside the second strip laid. I alternate directions and sides, working from the longest strips down to the shortest.

Once your lattice is laid, trim the edges of the crust to only slightly longer than the edge of the pie plate. Fold the bottom crust edge over the lattice edge, and pinch well to seal. Use your fingers to crimp/ruffle the edge of the pie. Carefully brush lattice and crust with whisked egg, and sprinkle with sugar.

Bake pie for 15 minutes at 425 F. Without opening the door, turn the temperature down to 400 F (200 C) and continue to bake for another 15 minutes or so.. until crust is golden.

Serve warm or cold – this pie is especially great with some rich vanilla ice cream on top.

* If you don't live somewhere that partridgeberries grow, you can ask around any Scandinavian shops and see if they know where you can find some. Alternatively, they can be purchased frozen online from some specialty retailers, and I'm told that IKEA sells them in their frozen section as well. (I just can't find anything on their site about it!)

Southern Comfort Peach Pie

Large ripe peaches	5	5
Southern Comfort	1/2 cup	125 ml
Fresh lemon juice	2 tsp	10 ml
Granulated sugar	3/4 cup	175 ml
Cornstarch	1/4 cup	50 ml
1 batch pie crust (Page 213)		
Large egg, whisked	1	1
Granulated sugar	2 Tbsp	30 ml

Peel peaches (optional), remove the pit and chop into chunks.

In a medium saucepan, combine 1/4 cup (50 ml) of the Southern Comfort, lemon juice, and sugar. Heat over low heat until mixture begins to simmer. Add about half of the chopped peaches, tossing to coat well with the liquid. Continue to cook for 5-10 minutes, or until peaches soften and start to break down a bit.

Mix remaining Southern Comfort with the corn starch, stirring until smooth with no lumps. Add to pot, stir until well incorporated. Add remaining peaches, continue to cook for 2 minutes. Remove from heat and allow to cool to room temperature.

Preheat oven to 425F (220 C)

Roll your two crusts out to about 1/4" thick. Line a pie pan with one crust, and cut the other into 1" strips. Transfer cooled filling into the pie shell, spreading to cover the bottom of the pie evenly.

Use the strips of pie crust to create a lattice on top. Once your lattice is laid, trim the edges of the crust to only slightly longer than the edge of the pie plate. Fold the bottom crust edge over the lattice edge, and pinch well to seal. Use your fingers to crimp/ruffle the edge of the pie. Carefully brush lattice and crust with whisked egg, and sprinkle with sugar.

Bake pie for 15 minutes. Without opening the door, turn the temperature down to 400 F (200 C) and continue to bake for another 15 minutes or so, until crust is golden. Serve warm or cold

Creamy Blueberry Amaretto Pie

This is the recipe that I worked out in a dream a few years ago. Lucid dreaming comes in handy sometimes - I tend to do a lot of problem solving and creative prep work while fast asleep. This isn't your traditional blueberry pie for two reasons:

- The introduction of Amaretto adds a new level of complexity to the filling.

- The addition of cream cheese makes the filling almost a cross between a blueberry pie and a cheesecake.

The creaminess works well with the Amaretto and blueberries, and this results in a well-structured pie that doesn't ooze all over the plate. (Once cooled, anyway!) It's delicious warm or cold, and is easy to make.

Cornstarch	1/4 cup	50 ml
Amaretto	1/4 cup	50 ml
Granulated sugar	3/4 cup	175 ml
Fresh blueberries	4 cups	1000 ml
Cream cheese, softened	8 oz	250 g
Amaretto	1/4 cup	50 ml
Large eggs	2	2
1 batch pie crust (Page 213)		
Large egg, beaten	1	1
Granulated sugar	2 Tbsp	30 ml

In a medium saucepan, combine cornstarch and Amaretto, whisking until smooth with no lumps. Add sugar, continuing to whisk until fully incorporated. Heat over medium-low heat until mixture begins to simmer. Add blueberries, tossing to coat well with the liquid. Continue to cook for 5 minutes.

Cream together cream cheese, Amaretto, and eggs until well incorporated and smooth. Stir into blueberry mixture. Heat, stirring frequently, until mixture comes just to a boil. Remove from heat, allow to cool to room temperature.

Preheat oven to 425 F (220 C)

Roll your two crusts out to about 1/4" thick. Line a pie pan with one crust, and cut the other into 1" strips.

Transfer cooled filling into the pie shell, spreading to cover the bottom of the pie evenly. Cover with remaining pie crust and pinch well to seal. Use your fingers to crimp/ruffle the edge of the pie. Carefully brush entire exposed crust with whisked egg, and sprinkle with sugar.

Bake pie for 15 minutes. Without opening the door, turn the temperature down to 400 F (200 C) and continue to bake for another 15 minutes or so.. until crust is golden. Serve warm or cold

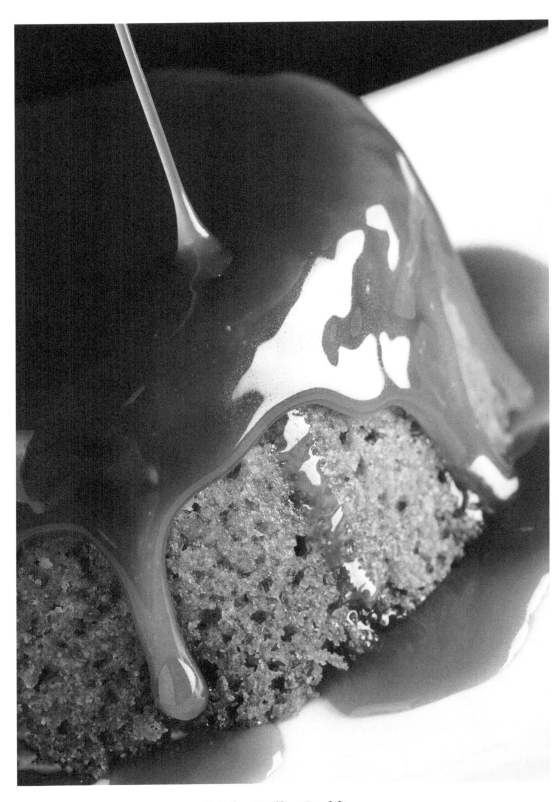

Sticky Toffee Pudding

Sticky Toffee Pudding

Sticky toffee pudding is a classic dessert in the UK, but a completely underutilized dessert option in North America - particularly in the USA. My own husband had never heard of it when I met him, and was surprised to see what it actually was. Rather than a common idea of a pudding in North America - a soft, custardy concoction, sticky toffee pudding is more of a gooey cake, steamed in a water bath.

Traditionally, these puddings tend to be prepared without the addition of booze in the toffee sauce. However, I AM the "Spirited Baker", and I do enjoy the added complexity that a little bit of a well-chosen spirit adds to the sauce. Rum, brandy, or whiskey tend to work the best for this, but be aware: whiskey is a spirit that is distilled from fermented wheat. While it doesn't cause a reaction in MOST people with gluten sensitivities - and the leading Celiac associations have deemed it gluten-free as of publication of this book - a few experts disagree. If you have noticed a reaction, or just want to play it extra safe, it could be a good idea forgo the whiskey in favour of rum or brandy.

Sorghum flour	1 cup	250 ml
Coconut flour	1/4 cup	50 ml
Brown rice flour	1/4 cup	50 ml
Salt	1 tsp	5 ml
Dates, pitted and finely chopped	1/2 lb	250 g
Water	1/2 cup	125 ml
Zest of 1 orange		
Baking soda	1/2 tsp	2 ml
Butter, softened	1/2 cup	125 ml
Brown sugar, packed	1 cup	250 ml
Vanilla extract	1 tsp	5 ml
Large eggs	3	3

Preheat oven to 350 F (180 C). Generously grease 8 6 oz ramekins, arrange in a 2"+ deep baking pan. Carefully pour water into the baking pan, until it reaches about halfway up the sides of the ramekins.

In a mixing bowl, combine flours and salt, set aside.

In a small saucepan, combine chopped dates, water, orange zest, and baking soda. Bring to a boil, stirring frequently. Allow to boil for 1 minute, remove from heat and allow to cool completely.

Cream butter and brown sugar until light and fluffy. Add vanilla and eggs, continue beating just until smooth. Add flour mixture, stirring just until combined. Gently fold in date mixture. Divide among prepared ramekins. Bake for 50-60 minutes, until knife inserted in center of the cakes comes out clean.

While waiting, make the toffee sauce:

Toffee Sauce

Butter	1/4 cup	50 ml
Heavy cream	1/2 cup	125 ml
Brown sugar, packed	1 1/4 cups	300 ml
rum, brandy, or whiskey*	1 Tbsp	15 ml
vanilla extract	1 tsp	5 ml

Melt butter in a medium saucepan. Add heavy cream and brown sugar, whisking until smooth. Bring to a boil over medium heat, stirring constantly. Boil for 3 minutes - stirring constantly - then remove from heat. Stir in booze of choice, and vanilla.

Serve warm, over sticky toffee puddings. These are particularly nice with a small amount of vanilla ice cream on top!

* You can skip this ingredient/ step, if you'd like.

Cheesecake

There are two main components to a cheesecake - the crust, and the "cake" itself. By varying the flavours involved in either or both of these elements, you're afforded an endless amount of dessert possibilities!

Basic Cheesecake Crust

Crumbs *	1 1/2 cup	375 ml
Granulated sugar	1/4 cup	50 ml
Butter, melted	5 Tbsp	75 ml

Combine all ingredients until completely incorporated & moistened. Evenly distribute across the bottom of a 9"spring form pan. Press ingredients firmly, extending crust partway up the sides of the pan. Chill for at least 1 hour.

* Crumbs:

- My default for gf crusts is to use nuts in place of the crumbs. You can vary which nut variety/varieties you use, mixing and matching to accent the cheesecake flavour. Almond is a nice, neutral flavour that pairs well with almost everything. Something like walnut is an earthier taste that pairs well with more robust flavoured cheesecakes.

- Any crispy (NOT chewy!) pre-packaged gluten free cookie can be used. Try gluten-free gingersnap cookies for a more flavourful crust, and to accent spicier cheesecakes (like pumpkin or chai!) Homemade cookies work well, too. Just make sure they're dried out first.

Basic Cheesecake Batter

Cream cheese, room temperature	2 lbs	1000 g
Granulated sugar	1 1/2 cup	375 ml
Sour cream	1 cup	250 ml
Heavy cream	1 cup	250 ml
Large eggs	6	6
Vanilla extract	1 Tbsp	15 ml
Juice of one lemon		

Preheat oven to 425 F   (220 C)

In stand mixer, beat together cream cheese and sugar until smooth. Add sour cream, heavy cream, eggs, vanilla extract and lemon juice. Beat on low / medium-low until smooth. Gently pour batter into prepared crust. Chill for 10 minutes.

Bake for 15 minutes. After 15 minutes, turn the oven down to 325 F (160 C) and bake for 50 minutes. Once baking time is complete, turn off the oven and allow cake to cool - WITHOUT opening the door! - for 2 hours. Chill cake thoroughly before serving.

Variations:

- Use a different extract in place of vanilla

- Use any cream liqueur in place of 1/2 cup (125 ml) of the heavy cream.

- Replace 1/2 cup (125 ml) of the heavy cream with fruit puree. Berries, pumpkin, even pureed canned lychees (drain them first) - your only limit is your imagination!

- Melt 8 oz of chocolate and add to the batter after beating it til smooth.

Brandied Apple Crisp

Apple crisp was the dish that I was first known for, back when I was a kid. I substituted my favorite granola cereal for the rolled oats that most recipes called for… and a favorite was born!

As an adult, I'm a big fan of the combination of apples, cinnamon, brown sugar, and apple brandy. The Apple Brandy gives a little extra something to this dish, an added warmth and complexity. It tastes like the holidays! This apple crisp is the perfect way to end a crisp, cool day of apple picking with your special someone.

Granulated sugar	1 1/2 cups	375 ml
Gluten-free oat flour	1 cup	250 ml
Sorghum flour	1/2 cup	125 ml
Gluten-free Granola*	2 cups	500 ml
Baking powder	1/2 tsp	2 ml
Baking soda	1/2 tsp	2 ml
Butter, melted	3/4 cup	175 ml
Large, tart apples	7-8	7-8
Apple brandy	1/3 cup	75 ml
Brown sugar, packed	1/2 cup	125 ml
Cinnamon	1/2 tsp	2 ml
Walnuts or almonds, optional	1/2 cup	125 ml

Preheat oven to 375 F (190 C). Grease a 9 x 13" baking dish, set aside.

In a medium bowl, combine sugar, flours, granola, baking powder and baking soda. Add melted butter, stir until well incorporated. Everything should be wet, but crumbly.

Peel (if you want – I don't usually), core, and chop the apples. Toss apple chunks with the apple brandy. Separately, combine brown sugar, cinnamon, and nuts – if using. Add to the bowl of apples, toss until apples are evenly coated.

Spread apple mixture evenly over the bottom of the baking dish. Top with an even layer of the granola mixture, patting down lightly. Bake for 35-45 minutes, or until topping is lightly browned, and apples are tender. Serve with ice cream or whipped cream.

* If you prefer, rolled oats can be substituted for the same amount of granola.

Variations:

- For a non alcoholic version, swap apple juice or apple cider

- Add sweetened dried cranberries instead of – or in addition to – the nuts.

- Add chopped up caramels in with the apples, before covering with streusel topping

Brandied Apple Crisp

Chai Cupcakes

Basic Vanilla Cake

As someone who has an entire cookbook dedicated to cake, I am pretty much obligated to include a cake recipe here! This is my basic gluten-free vanilla cake recipe, which can be customized many different ways.

Light buckwheat flour	1 1/4 cup	300 ml
Potato starch	1/3 cup	75 ml
Coconut flour	1/4 cup	50 ml
White rice flour	1/4 cup	50 ml
Granulated sugar	1 1/2 cup	375 ml
Baking powder	4 tsp	60 ml
Salt	1 tsp	15 ml
Instant vanilla pudding mix	3 ½ oz	96 g
Large eggs, separated	4	4
Water	1 1/3 cup	235 ml
Butter, melted	3/4 cup	175 ml

Preheat oven to 350 F (180 C) . Liberally grease two 8" round cake pans (or cupcake pans) with vegetable shortening, or line cupcake pan with paper liners.

Combine all of the dry ingredients in a large mixing bowl, set aside. Carefully separate eggs, placing yolks in the dry ingredients bowl along with water and melted butter. Whisk until smooth and well combined.

In a – very clean – mixing bowl or stand mixer, whip the egg whites on high speed, until stiff peaks form. Gently fold whipped egg whites into the main batter, until all of the "white" disappears.

Divide batter among prepared cake or cupcake pans (expect to get 18 cupcake cavities filled, only fill 2/3). Bake until golden and knife inserted into center of batter comes out clean and cake springs back – about 20-22 minutes for cupcakes, or about 35-40 minutes for cake rounds.

Allow to cool to room temperature before frosting.

Variations

Chocolate: Decrease buckwheat flour to 3/4 cup, add 1/2 cup cocoa powder to the dry mix

Citrus: Replace 1/2 cup of the water with fresh citrus juice of your choice, mixed with 1/4 tsp baking soda. Add zest of 1 lemon/lime/orange.

Chai: Add 2 Tbsp instant tea powder, 1 tsp cinnamon, 1 tsp ground cardamom, 1/2 tsp ground cloves, and 1/2 tsp nutmeg to the dry mix

American Buttercream

Butter, softened	1 cup	250 ml
Icing (powdered) sugar	2 lbs	1000 g
Milk	1/4 cup	50 ml
Vanilla extract	2 tsp	10 ml

Whip butter until smooth.

Slowly add powdered sugar a bit at a time, until fully incorporated. Beat on high for 1 minute – mixture will be very, very thick.

Lower mixer speed to lowest setting, and slowly add ½ of the milk. Beat until fully incorporated and smooth. Add flavoring, beating until smooth. Once incorporated, check for consistency. Add more milk or sugar to achieve the consistency you want or need.

Swiss Meringue Buttercream

Egg whites*	5	5
Sugar (NOT powdered!)	1 cup	250 ml
Unsalted butter	1 ½ cups	375 ml
Vanilla extract	2 tsp	10 ml

Mix egg whites and sugar in a very clean metal mixing bowl, and place over a pot of simmering water on your stove top. Whisk occasionally until it hits 160°F (72°C) on a candy thermometer.

Move egg mixture to your stand mixer and whip on high (using the whisk attachment) until stiff peaks form, and mixture is relatively cool. While waiting, cut up the butter into chunks.

When meringue has reached the stiff peaks stage, switch to low speed and add the butter a chunk at a time, continuing to mix until fully incorporated

Once butter is fully incorporated into the mix, turn speed back up to medium-high and whip until you have a smooth buttercream. It will go through some weird stages before this point – soupy, maybe curdled. Don't worry! It will come together! Add flavoring, continue to mix until well incorporated.

* Be VERY careful when separating your eggs. Even the slightest speck of egg yolk in the whites will prevent this frosting from properly whipping up!

Note: This frosting gets VERY hard if chilled. Always serve cakes at room temperature!

Brown Sugar Meringue Buttercream

Egg whites*	5	5
Brown Sugar, packed	1 cup	250 ml
Unsalted butter	1 ½ cups	375 ml
Vanilla extract	2 tsp	10 ml

Mix egg whites and brown sugar in a very clean metal mixing bowl, and place over a pot of simmering water on your stove top. Whisk occasionally until it hits 160°F (72°C) on a candy thermometer.

Move egg mixture to your stand mixer and whip on high (using the whisk attachment) until stiff peaks form, and mixture is relatively cool. While waiting, cut up the butter into chunks.

When meringue has reached the stiff peaks stage, switch to low speed and add the butter a chunk at a time. Add flavoring, continuing to mix until fully incorporated

Once butter and flavoring are incorporated into the mix, turn speed back up to high and whip until you have a smooth buttercream. It will go through some weird stages before this point – soupy, maybe curdled. Don't worry! It will come together!

* As with all meringue recipes, be VERY careful when separating your eggs. Even the slightest speck of egg yolk in the whites will prevent this frosting from properly whipping up!

Note: This frosting gets VERY hard if chilled. Always serve cakes at room temperature!

Cream Cheese Frosting

Butter, softened	1/4 cup	50 ml
Cream cheese, softened	8 oz	250 g
Icing (powdered) sugar	1- 2 lbs	500-1000 g
Milk	2 Tbsp	30 ml
Vanilla Extract	2 tsp	10 ml

Whip butter and cream cheese together until smooth and fluffy. Slowly add powdered sugar a bit at a time, until fully incorporated. Beat on high for 1 minute – mixture will be very, very thick.

Lower mixer speed to lowest setting, and slowly add ½ of the milk. Beat until fully incorporated and smooth. Add vanilla extract, beating until smooth. Once incorporated, check for consistency. Add more milk or sugar to achieve the consistency you want or need.

Stabilized Whipped Cream

This frosting is a nice, less-sweet frosting. It is particularly nice with lighter cakes, and with fruit. This can be used as a filling, frosting, and piped for decorating - just be sure to keep the cake chilled!

Unflavored gelatin powder	2 tsp	10 ml
Cold Water	3 Tbsp	45 ml
Heavy whipping cream	2 cups	500 ml
Icing (powdered) Sugar	1/2 cup	125 ml
Flavor extract	1/2-1 tsp	2-5 ml

Sprinkle gelatin over the cold water in a small bowl and let it absorb for five minutes.

Combine heavy whipping cream, powdered sugar, and flavor extract in a mixing bowl. Whip until soft peaks start to form.

Transfer gelatin mixture to the microwave. Heat in 10 second increments until the gelatin dissolves into the water.

Fold gelatin mixture to cream mixture, then whip until stiff peaks form.

Conversions

To accommodate bakers in different countries and from different cultures, measurements throughout this book have been provided in both U.S. conventional and metric. To keep things simple, measurement conversions have been rounded. See below for the exact conversions, as well as the rounded versions provided throughout this book.

Spoons	Actual Conversion*	Standard Metric Used
1/4 tsp	1.2 ml	1 ml
½ tsp	2.5 ml	2 ml
1 tsp	4.9 ml	5 ml
1 Tbsp	14.8 ml	15 ml

Cups	Actual Conversion*	Standard Metric Used
1/4 cup	59.1 ml	50 ml
1/3 cup	78.9 ml	75 ml
½ cup	118.3 ml	125 ml
2/3 cup	157.7 ml	150 ml
3/4 cup	177.4 ml	175 ml
1 cup	236.6 ml	250 ml
4 cups	946.4 ml	1000 ml / 1 liter

Ounces (Weight)	Actual Conversion*	Standard Metric Used
1 oz	28.3 grams	30 grams
2 oz	56.7 grams	55 grams
3 oz	85.0 grams	85 grams
4 oz	113.4 grams	125 grams
5 oz	141.7 grams	140 grams
6 oz	170.1 grams	170 grams
7 oz	198.4 grams	200 grams
8 oz	226.8 grams	250 grams
16 oz / 1 lb	453.6 grams	500 grams
32 oz / 2 lbs	907.2 grams	1000 grams / 1 kilogram

* Source: Google Calculator

Resources

This list is for informational purposes only, and does not necessarily constitute an endorsement of any of these companies. We do not receive payment of any kind by these companies for being listed here. It is the readers' responsibility to properly vet any companies they choose to do business with; we are not responsible for any disputes that may arise.

Ingredients

Futter's Nut Butters
www.futtersnutbutters.com
Various all natural nut butters - Great for filling macarons!

Nuts Online
www.nutsonline.com
Gluten-free flours, nuts, dried fruits, fruit powders, and more.

Purcell Mountain Farms
www.purcellmountainfarms.com
Red & blue cornmeal, other dry ingredients

Equipment

Amazon
www.amazon.com

Other

Celebration Generation
www.celebrationgeneration.com
Food & lifestyle blog, recipes, photos, and inspiration

Index

Marie Porter

Marie Porter is an award winning cake artist and costume designer based in Minnesota's Twin Cities. Known as much for her delicious and diverse flavour menu as for her sugar artistry, Marie's work has graced magazines and blogs around the world.

Marie is the author of the"The Spirited Baker", "Evil Cake Overlord" and "Sweet Corn Spectacular" cookbooks, as well as a line of six sewing manuals.

Marie also maintains a food / lifestyle blog, "Celebration Generation"

Michael Porter

Michael Porter works in medical manufacturing, and is a food and commercial photographer. His work has appeared in local, national, and international magazines, in catalogs, corporate websites, and as well as in many online media outlets.

In addition to being an awesome husband and photographer, Michael is Celebration Generation's "Chief Engineering Officer", responsible for all custom builds, equipment repairs, and warp engine emergencies. After their home was smashed by a tornado, Michael singlehandedly built all of the cabinetry in their new kitchen!

MARIE PORTER

TWISTED

A MINNEAPOLIS
TORNADO MEMOIR

Twisted: A Minneapolis Tornado Memoir

On the afternoon of May 22, 2011, North Minneapolis was devastated by a tornado. Twisted recounts the Porters' first 11 months, post tornado. Rebuilding their house, working around the challenges presented by inadequate insurance coverage. Frustration at repeated bouts of incompetence and greed from their city officials. Dealing with issues such as loss of control, logistics, change, and over-stimulation, as two adults with Aspergers. With the help of social media – and the incredibly generous support of the geek community – the Porters were able to emerge from the recovery marathon without too much of a hit to their sanity levels. New friends were made, new skills learned, and a "new" house emerged from the destruction. Twisted is a roller coaster of emotion, personal observations, rants, humour, social commentary, set backs and triumphs. Oh, and details on how to cook jambalaya for almost 300 people, in the parking lot of a funeral home... should you ever find yourself in the position to do so!

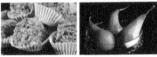

The Spirited Baker

Combining liqueurs with more traditional baking ingredients can yield spectacular results. Try Mango Mojito Upside Down Cake, Candy Apple Flan, Jalapeno Beer Peanut Brittle, Lynchburg Lemonade Cupcakes, Pina Colada Rum Cake, Strawberry Daiquiri Chiffon Pie, and so much more.

To further add to your creative possibilities, the first chapter teaches how to infuse spirits to make both basic and cream liqueurs, as well as home made flavour extracts! This book contains over 160 easy to make recipes, with variation suggestions to help create hundreds more!

Sweet Corn Spectacular

The height of summer brings with it the bounty of fresh sweet corn. Grilled or boiled, slathered in butter and sprinkled with salt, corn on the cob is a mainstay of cook-out menus. But this "vegetable" can grace your plate in so many other ways. In fact, author and baker Marie Porter once devised an entire day's worth of corn-based dishes to celebrate her "corn freak" husband's birthday.   *Sweet Corn Spectacular* displays Porter's creative and flavour-filled approach to this North American original, inspiring   year-round use of this versatile ingredient and tasty experimenting in your own kitchen. As Porter reminds home cooks, the possibilities are endless!

Evil Cake Overlord

Marie Porter has been known for her "ridiculously delicious" moist cakes and tasty, unique flavors since the genesis of her custom cake business. Now, you can have recipes for all of the amazing flavors on her former custom cake menu, as well as many more! Once you have baked your moist work of gastronomic art, fill and frost your cake with any number of tasty possibilities. Milk chocolate cardamom pear, mango mojito.. even our famous Chai cake – the flavor that got us into "Every Day with Rachel Ray" magazine! Feeling creative? Use our easy to follow recipe to make our yummy fondant. Forget everything you've heard about fondant – ours is made from marshmallows and powdered sugar, and is essentially candy – you can even flavor it to bring a whole new level of "yum!" to every cake you make!

For wholesale inquiries or to purchase directly, visit

www.celebrationgeneration.com

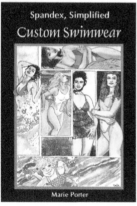

CPSIA information can be obtained at www.ICGtesting.com
Printed in the USA
BVOW11s2104140914

366508BV00008B/9/P